W9-BBM-995

JOSÉ CLEMENTE OROZCO

Mexican Artist

Bárbara C. Cruz

Enslow Publishers, Inc.

40 Industrial Road PO Box 38
Box 398 Aldershot
Berkeley Heights, NJ 07922 Hants GU12 6BP
USA UK

http://www.enslow.com

For my sister and brother, Iliana and Eddy,
each artists in their own way

Library of Congress Cataloging-in-Publication Data

Cruz, Bárbara.
    José Clemente Orozco : Mexican artist / Bárbara C. Cruz.
       p. cm. — (Hispanic biographies)
    Includes bibliographical references and index.
    Summary: Discusses the life and times of José Clemente Orozco, who
has been called "the most original and powerful mural painter" in
Mexico despite having been badly injured in an explosion as a teenager.
    ISBN 0-7660-1041-4
    1. Orozco, José Clemente, 1883–1949—Juvenile literature.
    2. Painters—Mexico—Biography—Juvenile literature. [1. Orozco,
José Clemente, 1883–1949. 2. Artists.] I. Title. II. Series.
ND259.07C78   1998
760'.092—dc21
[B]   98-26414
                                       CIP
                                       AC

Printed in the United States of America

10 9 8 7 6 5 4 3

Illustration Credits: Enslow Publishers, Inc., pp. 12, 76; INBA,
Mexico, pp. 14, 16, 19, 37, 54, 67, 79, 81, 88, 90, 97, 102, 104;
Bárbara C. Cruz, pp. 41, 48, 50, 85, 111; The New School for Social
Research, p. 70.

Cover Illustration: Center for Creative Photography, University of
Arizona.

CONTENTS

Acknowledgments   5

1   Tragedy at a Young Age   7

2   The Blossoming Artist. 11

3   ¡Revolución!. 23

4   Mexico's Golden Age 34

5   El Norte 56

6   The Artist in New England. 72

7   Back Home 83

8   A Productive Life 93

9   His Legacy, His Art 106

Chronology 115

Chapter Notes 118

Further Reading 125

Index 126

ACKNOWLEDGMENTS

Without the help and support of the following people, this book would have been impossible:

Jack Vine, whose initial enthusiastic feedback inspired me to keep going;

Jennifer Groendal, who relentlessly unearthed data in the USF library;

Ward Stavig, El Rey de las Albondigas Noruegas, who patiently researched and answered questions at a moment's notice;

Señoritas Claudia Irán Jasso Apango, Cristina García Hernández, y Cristina Hijar González at the Centro Nacional de las Artes in Mexico City, for their assistance and courtesy; the anonymous reviewers who provided excellent insight and suggestions; and finally, Kevin and Cristina Yelvington, whose constant support and affection were invaluable in the realization of this project.

TRAGEDY AT A
YOUNG AGE

The year was 1897 and José Clemente Orozco was fourteen years old. Clemente, as he was called, and his family lived in one of the oldest and most charming neighborhoods in Mexico City. Most of the streets were paved with cobblestones. Because the old Aztec lake Texcoco had not yet been fully drained, the old quarter of the city had a network of canals and waterways that Clemente would walk alongside on his way to school.

Clemente's family sent him to the National School of Agriculture in nearby San Jacinto to prepare him for a career in soil management and the raising of crops.

Clemente was not especially interested in agriculture, however, and was slowly realizing that his true love was drawing and painting.[1]

Like many other boys his age, Clemente was curious about the firecrackers and gunpowder that were used to celebrate during Mexico's many festive holidays. One leisurely day at home when school was not in session, Clemente decided to conduct a chemistry experiment involving gunpowder. Suddenly, without Clemente's knowing what was happening, the gunpowder exploded. Three fingers from his left hand were completely blown off; his right hand was badly shattered. Orozco's parents quickly called a doctor to the house. The doctor, realizing the severity of the accident, immediately sent the teenage boy to San Lázaro Hospital in Mexico City.

As soon as the surgeon saw the damage and the infection that had already set in, he realized that the left hand would have to be amputated. After evaluating the damage on Clemente's right hand, the doctor feared he would have to amputate it as well. A servant who had been with the family for many years intervened and prevented the amputation from taking place.

Clemente's right hand was saved but would show deep scars for the rest of his life. His left hand was completely removed as was most of the wrist. Clemente's eyes and ears were also hurt in the explosion. His vision and hearing were permanently affected.

Clemente would never be able to hear out of his left ear again and would have to wear thick glasses for the rest of his life.

Later, when he was asked about the accident, Clemente dismissed it with a shrug, saying: "I was just playing in the street with some powder. It was just an ordinary explosion."[2] He denied reports that he had been conducting an elaborate experiment in a chemical laboratory.

For most people, such a devastating accident would perhaps erase any dream of becoming an artist. However, Clemente was not like most people. He soon learned how to do everything with one hand—tie his shoelaces, chop wood, and even draw and paint. He was resolved to not let his disability stand in the way of his ambition.

THE BLOSSOMING ARTIST

José Clemente Orozco was born in the Mexican coastal state of Jalisco on November 23, 1883. Ciudad Guzmán, the city of his birth, was a quaint town with a rich Indian heritage. The locals called the city by its Indian name, Zapotlán el Grande.

Clemente's father, Ireneo Orozco, owned several factories that produced soap, inks, and dyes. Clemente's mother, Rosa Flores, had an interest in all the arts, but she especially enjoyed painting and music. Unfortunately, Ireneo's printing plant did not do well and the family was forced to move to Guadalajara, the capital of Jalisco, when Clemente was not yet three

Mexico

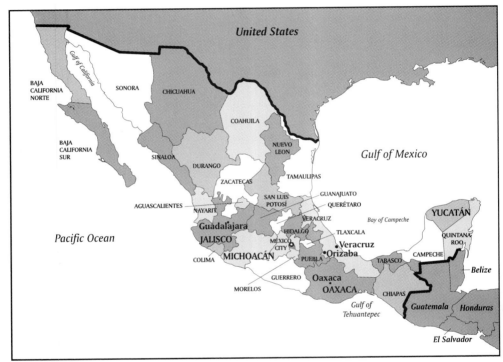

United States

Gulf of California

BAJA CALIFORNIA NORTE

SONORA

CHICUAHUA

COAHUILA

BAJA CALIFORNIA SUR

SINALOA

DURANGO

NUEVO LEON

Gulf of Mexico

ZACATECAS

TAMAULIPAS

AGUASCALIENTES

NAYARIT

SAN LUIS POTOSÍ

GUANAJUATO

QUERÉTARO

YUCATÁN

Guadalajara

VERACRUZ

Bay of Campeche

JALISCO

HIDALGO

TLAXCALA

QUINTANA ROO

Pacific Ocean

MÉXICO CITY

Veracruz

COLIMA

MICHOACÁN

Orizaba

PUEBLA

TABASCO

CAMPECHE

Belize

GUERRERO

Oaxaca

MORELOS

OAXACA

CHIAPAS

Gulf of Tehuantepec

Guatemala

Honduras

El Salvador

José Clemente Orozco was born in the Mexican coastal state of Jalisco.

years old. They moved into Rosa's family home where she herself had grown up. Since her family was wealthy and distinguished, the house was a beautiful one facing the temple of San Felipe.

The family lived there until 1890 when they moved to Mexico City. There they lived in the oldest *barrio* in the city. Their neighborhood had a maze of waterways and canals. That same year, Clemente was enrolled in the *Escuela Primaria* (Primary School) that was part of the Teachers' College. By that time, Clemente had just turned six, his sister, Rosa, was a few years older, and his brother, Luis, was still an infant.

As a boy in grade school, Clemente was a quiet, thoughtful child who rarely took part in rough games. To amuse himself and his friends, he spent many hours drawing *muñecos*, funny figures that made the other children laugh. A classmate of Clemente's remembers him this way: "Clemente was a quiet, introspective boy. He was always neatly, though inexpensively, dressed. He was very well behaved and we all knew that he had a great heart."[1]

When Clemente was ten years old, he discovered the printmaking of José Guadalupe Posada. By using an inked type and printing press, printmakers at the turn of the century kept the public informed of the latest news, entertainment, and articles for sale. Posada is considered the father of Mexican printmaking and is often called "the printmaker of the people."[2] The

Clemente's parents, Rosa Flores de Orozco and Ireneo Orozco, on their wedding day.

former schoolteacher made prints that criticized the government, corrupt politicians, and greedy business-men in much the same way political cartoons do today.

Most of these cartoons were printed on bright yellow, magenta, or green paper and sold for just a penny on street corners. Shoeless young boys would shout the most scandalous headlines to tempt people to buy the penny sheets. Sometimes the young Clemente could not resist and would spend his small allowance on Posada's papers.[3]

Posada's workshop was on a cobblestoned street, very close to Clemente's school. As a young boy, Clemente watched Posada engraving plates, either in his print shop window or in an open stall on the street. Since Clemente went home for lunch, like all his schoolmates, he went by Posada's shop four times a day. Posada first stimulated Clemente's interest in drawing.[4]

While Clemente was attending grade school, he learned of night classes that were being offered at the government-sponsored Academy of Fine Arts of San Carlos. Clemente begged his mother to take him to the academy until she finally agreed. When his mother sat down with the academy's director, she was told that at six years of age, Clemente was too young to be a student there. But Clemente's mother persisted, convinced of her son's talent. Finally, the director

Orozco spent his first three years in Ciudad Guzmán, before the family moved to Mexico City. Pictured above is the artist at age one.

agreed to admit the young boy but without formal enrollment.[5]

While he attended his regular school during the day, Clemente went to art classes at the San Carlos Academy at night. At first, Clemente was left by himself in the back of the classroom, ignored by the instructor and his fellow students. One evening, the instructor happened to look over Clemente's shoulder and was amazed at what he saw. He conveyed his astonishment to the director, who promptly called Clemente's mother. Doña Rosa was pleased to hear that her young son not only drew better than many of his older class-mates but also, in the estimation of the director, drew better than many of the academy's teachers![6]

After Clemente finished grammar school, his family sent him to the National School of Agriculture in San Jacinto to prepare him for a career in soil management and the raising of crops. Clemente's parents felt that this training would provide him with steady work as an adult. Although Clemente was not interested in agri-culture, the training he received came in handy at his first paid job: drawing topographical maps. These maps show the surface features of a place or region. Later as an adult, Clemente recalled his three years in the country as "healthy and happy"[7] despite the fact that it was during this time that he was disfigured by the gunpowder explosion. He also developed a heart condition that would trouble him for years to come.

Clemente graduated from the National School of Agriculture in 1899 with a degree in agricultural engineering.

Clemente then chose to enter the National Preparatory School in 1900, specializing in the study of mathematics and architectural drawing. "La Prepa," as it was called by its students, was Mexico's top school for preparing students for university study. Clemente was a good student and maintained high marks in all his subjects.

Toward the end of his schooling at La Prepa, Clemente's father died of typhoid fever. His father's death, coupled with Clemente's gunpowder accident, put a financial strain on the family. To pay for the night classes at the San Carlos Academy, Clemente took a part-time job in an architect's office. By working as an architect's draftsman for architect Carlos Herrera, Clemente was able to pay his way through school.

When Clemente first enrolled at the San Carlos Art Academy, students there were taught in traditional ways. At the time, the favorite method of instruction was for students to copy European prints and paintings. In particular, they were taught to duplicate the work of the Renaissance masters, such as da Vinci. Sometimes students were faced with the same model for weeks or even months at a time. Their goal was to copy nature with the photographic exactness that was favored at the time by European academics. At the end

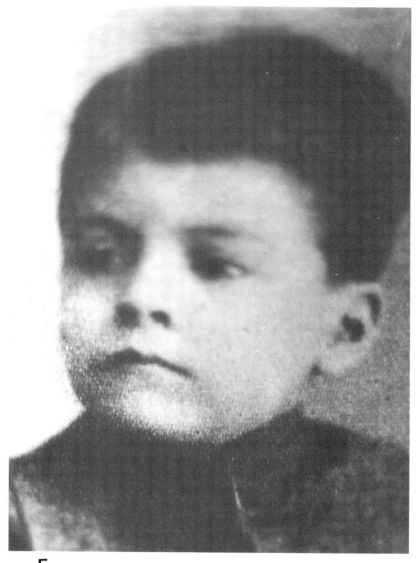

Even as a young child, Orozco showed great artistic ability.
Here he is at age four.

of the pose, a photographer was called in to take a picture. The students would then compare their drawings against this photograph.[8] During the turn of the century, native Mexican art was considered inferior while that of Europe was praised. Clemente complained of his instructors: "They let us paint, but we had to paint the way they did in Paris."[9]

During this time, Clemente met Gerardo Murillo, who was teaching at the academy. Murillo was better known to his fellow Mexicans as Dr. Atl. He had changed his name as a young man to the Aztec word for water (atl) in part to show his respect for Mexico's Indian cultures and in part to show his scorn for the Spanish, who had conquered Mexico through force. A native of Guadalajara, Dr. Atl achieved recognition as an artist and revolutionary. Soon after the two met, they became friends. The colorful Dr. Atl told the young artist all about the magnificent frescoes (paintings on walls and ceilings) that he had seen in Rome. He also shared with Clemente his political and philosophical ideas, which were critical of the government and in support of workers and peasants. Dr. Atl continued his spontaneous lectures off campus, where he invited Clemente and other young artists to share a meal of home-cooked spaghetti with meat sauce.[10] Later, Clemente fondly remembered the *macaroni à la Italiana*, which Dr. Atl cooked up in empty oil cans.[11]

After a while, Dr. Atl became Clemente's artistic mentor and political tutor.

In 1910, an all-Mexican art show was held at the Academy of San Carlos to coincide with the Centennial of the *Grito de Dolores* (Cry of Dolores). This celebration marked the day in 1810 when Mexico revolted against Spain. Orozco was invited by his professors to display some of his work. He chose some of his charcoal drawings and cartoons. In the official chronicle of the show, Orozco's early drawings were described as "bold and firm, supremely expressive and full of very deep intentions" and compared with the drawings of the famous French artist Rodin.[12]

Clemente's future in art was looking very bright.

CHAPTER THREE

¡REVOLUCIÓN!

By 1910, living conditions for many Mexicans had become very difficult. Despite Mexico's revolt from Spain one hundred years earlier, most of the Mexican patriots' goals had not yet been achieved. Although President Porfirio Díaz had built railroads and brought some economic progress to the country, life for most workers and peasants was very harsh.

In his drive for growth and power, Díaz crushed anyone who disagreed with him and gave away many of Mexico's natural resources. Eventually, these hard and unfair conditions led to an armed rebellion and revolution that began in 1910. The civil war, which followed the beginning of the revolution, would last ten years and would prove to be one of the bloodiest periods in Mexican history. Nearly 2 million Mexicans lost their lives, most of them innocent peasants who were caught in the crossfire between government supporters and peasant revolutionaries.

At first, Orozco volunteered to fight with the revolutionaries, but he was turned away because he was an amputee. Shortly after the Mexican Revolution erupted in November 1910, Orozco found work as a newspaper cartoonist. Mexico has a strong tradition of satirical political cartoons, and many people learned of the issues pertinent to the revolution through them. Orozco's first cartoons were for a newspaper called *El Hijo del Ahuizote* (The Son of the Ahuizote). The name of the newspaper came from the Aztec legend of a monster that lured sailors to their death with its voice. He produced many prints and etchings that tackled the major issues of the day.

In his free time, Orozco began experimenting with watercolor and oil painting. When he started painting, Orozco expressed disgust at the pretty, sunlit school of painting that was popular at the time.[1] While most of his fellow artists were imitating French techniques like Impressionism, Orozco decided to take a riskier route. He later wrote in his autobiography, "I preferred to paint in black and in the earth colors that had been excluded from the Impressionist palette. Instead of red and yellow twilight, I painted the pestilent [plagued] shadows of closed rooms, and instead of the male Indian, drunken ladies and gentlemen."[2]

In June 1911, students at the San Carlos Academy staged a strike. The art students were unhappy with the director, Antonio Rivas Mercado, who was a strict supporter of European painting. During the strike, the teenage art students asked their older fellow student, Orozco, to give them his advice. Orozco worked tirelessly to resolve the conflict.

Finally, in 1913, Alfredo Ramos Martínez was appointed as director to replace Mercado. Martínez was influenced by the thoughts and goals of the Impressionists. The Impressionist artists believed that every human being is born with the ability to receive impressions from the outside world, interpret them individually, and express those impressions in a spontaneous manner. Ramos Martínez adapted this philosophy to his new job: He said that his goal was to promote self-pride in his art students, pointing to the beauty of Mexico and the development of a national art form.[3]

From 1911 to 1913, Orozco spent a lot of time in Mexico City's segregated district studying the impoverished and down-on-their-luck citizens. In the "wretchedest *barrios* [neighborhoods] in the city," as Orozco later called them, he was in a good position to study the poor residents. In this section of the capital, there were several brothels, or houses of prostitution. Orozco observed the hard lives that the women endured. In 1913, he produced most of the studies that would later become part of a series of watercolor paintings entitled *House of Tears*. These melancholy watercolors of prostitutes portrayed the women sensitively, showing the many hardships that they faced. Orozco also showed them during their off-hours—dancing, yawning, stretching, and chatting. He later told a friend that when the lonely women saw him coming, they would cry out "Here comes Jesuito!" and would welcome him warmly, because he was the only person who would listen to them and give them sound advice.[4]

That same year, Orozco painted a canvas for the Museum of San Juan de Ulúa in Veracruz. This oil painting, which was later hung in the lobby, was Orozco's first government commission. In *Surrender by the Spaniards at San Juan de Ulúa in 1822*, he depicted the retreat and surrender of the Spanish Army during an attack on the fort of San Juan de Ulúa. When art critic José Juan Tablada saw Orozco's work, he declared, "José Clemente Orozco is a strong artist, very intense, very personal, and eminently distinguished."[5]

In 1913 President Madero was assassinated by General Victoriano Huerta, a supporter of former President Porfirio Díaz. A year later, Huerta was forced out of office by Venustiano Carranza, a former member of Huerta's government who supported giving land to the peasants. Carranza soon appointed Dr. Atl, who was one of his supporters, as the San Carlos Art Academy's director. It was largely under the influence of Dr. Atl that Orozco began to sympathize with the politics of Carranza.[6] Orozco soon joined Carranza's Constitutionalists who were supposedly fighting on behalf of the Mexican masses to improve their living conditions.

In 1915, Carranza was defeated by the legendary peasant revolutionaries Pancho Villa and Emiliano Zapata. When the Carranza forces were forced to retreat from the capital city, Orozco joined them. Dr. Atl, who was also in the group, established the pro-Carranza daily newspaper *La Vanguardia*. Orozco was hired as the newspaper's caricaturist.

As the political cartoonist for *La Vanguardia*, Orozco traveled in a railroad car along with the revolutionary soldiers. He worked in one of the railroad cars, which had been converted into an editorial office. At night he slept on a military cot. On many mornings Orozco was awakened by the sound of guns firing during the dawn executions.

As Orozco followed the army from town to town, the budding artist gathered his impressions of the revolution. He saw men hanged from telegraph poles, firing squads carrying out their grisly task, mutilated soldiers, and mobile hospitals leaving behind amputated arms and legs. Later, Orozco would capture some of these experiences in paintings, drawings, and murals.

Orozco became disillusioned at the excesses of political power, even among the revolutionary forces, as he witnessed large-scale executions and the looting of churches.[7] While many artists represented the positive aims of the revolution and Mexico's bright future, Orozco starkly highlighted the death and despair. His cartoons became increasingly disparaging of the revolution.

Orozco's caricatures were said to "strike the eye at once with their originality, vigor, and ferocity."[8] Because they were so bold and honest, Orozco's caricatures were not received well by Carranza's party. The cartoons were considered too graphic a portrayal of the looting and horror of the war.[9]

While in Orizaba, Orozco met sixteen-year-old Margarita Valladares. The youngest daughter of a well-known family in Oaxaca, the dark-eyed, dark-haired Margarita was a pretty, quiet, serious young woman. Dr. Atl hired Margarita and her two sisters, Estela and Hortensia, to fold copies of *La Vanguardia*.

Dr. Atl arranged for several dinners where Margarita happened to be seated directly across from Orozco. Her hands were so beautiful that Orozco asked her to pose for him for a study of hands he was drawing. During the sitting, the artist and Margarita made pleasant small talk about life in Orizaba. Orozco was charmed by Margarita but was too shy to tell her his feelings. In addition to being almost twice her age, he also felt ashamed of his disabled body. Orozco described the love he felt for Margarita as "violent, painful, and without hope."[10] He decided to leave Orizaba and concentrate instead on his art.

In 1916, Orozco left Orizaba and returned to Mexico City. He gained fame with the sharp, satirical cartoons that he continued to draw for various newspapers. To sell more newspapers, paperboys would open their paper at the page that had Orozco's drawing. At the top of their lungs, they cried out the day's headlines and provoked the public's curiosity. Some art historians feel that this early career as a political caricaturist would have the most lasting impact on Orozco's art, since he used satire in virtually all his work.[11]

In September of that year, Orozco had his first public, one-man exhibition in the Librería Biblos bookstore. Originally it had been scheduled for the gallery of the Casa Francisco Navarro, but the owner was concerned about the subject matter of the artwork and the exhibition was moved to the bookstore at the last minute. The show was made up of 123 drawings and paintings of women and schoolgirls as well as some political cartoons. Of all his paintings, the ones that drew the most attention were part of the *House of Tears* series, which depicted the city's prostitutes in a variety of dark and somber settings.

For the most part, though, the *House of Tears* series was not received well. It was a conservative time and people were enraged and shocked that an immoral activity such as prostitution would be displayed so openly. Others also criticized Orozco's painting as sloppy, his technique as second-rate, and his drawing as incompetent.[12]

Even though the show brought Orozco an avalanche of criticism, the display eventually had a profound influence on modern art in Mexico.[13] One art critic who defended Orozco was José Juan Tablada. He appreciated Orozco's realistic interpretations, writing, "so far Orozco has been the sharpest observer of certain classes in Mexico City and all other Mexican urban centers."[14] Another writer felt that it was Orozco's direct contact with people that made his art so perceptive.[15]

Despite these supporters, Orozco was stung by the sharp criticism. The rejection that Orozco felt following his first one-man show hurt the artist deeply and pushed him into a period of inactivity.[16] He even published a response to the criticism in a local paper. He wrote: "I live in misery. Each sheet of paper, each tube of paint, is for me a sacrifice and a sadness. Is it fair to subject me to scorn and hostility and furthermore to insult me publicly?"[17]

However, the artist was far from putting his paints and brushes away permanently. In 1917 Orozco began to produce a series of watercolors using the revolution as his theme. Rather than glorify the revolution, as most other Mexican artists were doing, Orozco painted the ugly sides of war. With bloody images still fresh in his mind, he painted exhausted soldiers, weeping women, the maimed and dead victims of the war. He depicted humans as destructive, savage beasts. He kept these watercolors mostly to himself, however, and dreamed of a place where his work might be received more positively.

Orozco had always wanted to visit the United States. He imagined a public that would be more open and receptive to his art. In 1917, he set off to El Norte, as the United States is sometimes called in Mexico. Orozco crossed into the United States through the border town of Laredo, Texas. Rather than the open reception he had envisioned, the artist was detained by American customs officials over the content of his artwork. When the customs officials reviewed Orozco's one hundred-plus watercolors and drawings, they claimed that the art was offensive, lewd, and immoral. Orozco protested, saying that the pictures were far from immoral, that there was nothing shameless about them, and that the figures were not even nude.[18]

The officials, however, would not budge on their position and confiscated a number of his watercolors.

Orozco was speechless when they proceeded to rip into bits more than sixty of the watercolors. Troubled, the artist continued on his trip to San Francisco, hoping that things would go better there.

Orozco arrived in San Francisco in the midst of World War I. It was an animated place. He was amazed at the sights and sounds of Chinatown, the Bohemian neighborhoods, the many tattoo parlors catering to sailors, and the fantastic forests just outside the city.

He was soon introduced to Fernando R. Galván. Orozco and Galván decided to go into business together producing posters for movie houses. Using cheap materials, they divided a workshop on Mission Street into living quarters, an office, a carpenter's shop, and a studio. Outside they hung their sign: FERNANDO R. GALVAN & COMPANY. Orozco wryly noted that all by himself, he was the "Company."[19]

Galván and Orozco soon received their first order: to assemble hand-painted announcements of upcoming films for movie theaters. Orozco painted the announcements and Galván made the frames. They later received other jobs tinting and enlarging portrait photographs. Although it was going well, Orozco became bored and longed to further his career in art. He decided to try his luck in New York City.

Fellow Mexican artist David Alfaro Siqueiros, who was in New York at the time with his new bride, visited

Orozco in 1919. Siqueiros recalled his friend's meager living conditions: "He lived in extreme poverty, working in a doll factory, painting the complexions with an airbrush and the eyes and lashes by hand."[20]

The one bright spot in Orozco's life during his time in New York were the fantastic art museums he visited, such as the Museum of Modern Art, and his visits to Harlem and Coney Island. At the Museum of Modern Art in New York, Orozco studied the paintings of famous artists like Picasso, Matisse, and Chirico.

Despite these amusements, Orozco missed his homeland. In 1920, the peacefully elected Alvaro Obregón took office as president of Mexico and the ten years of civil war ended. The artist also learned that mural painting and folk art were gaining popularity back home. After two years in the United States, Orozco decided it was time to return to Mexico.

MEXICO'S
GOLDEN AGE

Upon his return to Mexico in 1920, José Clemente Orozco set up a studio for himself in Coyoacán, a suburb of Mexico City. Orozco immediately found work as a newspaper illustrator. Although the Mexican Revolution was now officially over, the artist soon reestablished his reputation with his sharp cartoons lampooning corrupt and incompetent politicians. When he was not working as a political cartoonist, Orozco continued to experiment with watercolor and oil painting.

After his return from the United States, where he had visited many art museums, Orozco continued to learn more about international art. During the summer of 1922, Orozco attended lectures at the San Carlos Academy given by Walter Pach, a visiting professor and art critic from the United States. Professor Pach recalled that Orozco was his most devoted student.[1] Orozco also became reacquainted with Margarita Valladares, whom he had met in 1915 when he was in Orizaba. Both of them lived in Coyoacán and took the train into Mexico City where they both worked. Whenever they bumped into each other, Orozco would respectfully tip his hat in her direction. One day Orozco took Margarita's sister, Hortensia, aside and revealed his love for Minita, as he called Margarita. Hortensia urged him to visit her sister at the family home. Orozco and Margarita soon began a courtship that would last two years.

Orozco waited for Margarita every day after work, and they walked together to the train that took them from the Zócalo back home to Coyoacán. On Sundays the two would go on long walks and go to the movies, which although they did not yet have sound, entertained Margarita and Orozco.[2]

Margarita's friends could not understand what she saw in the solemn artist. They would tell her, "Orozco is so serious and severe-looking! You're going to have a hard time understanding him!" Margarita merely replied, "It is precisely his seriousness that I like best. With me he's very affectionate and besides, his sober personality gives me a feeling of security."[3] As his love for the young woman deepened, Orozco began to send Minita love letters. What he was too shy to say in person, he put down on paper: "I love you. I adore you madly, blindly, with delirium, with all my soul, with my whole being. I love you, beautiful Margarita!"[4]

During this period, Orozco joined the Syndicate of Revolutionary Technical Workers, Painters, and Sculptors, uniting with acclaimed painters such as Diego Rivera, David Alfaro Siqueiros, and other young artists. The artists created this trade union to represent them in their dealings with the government. The organization's manifesto, *Social, Political, and Aesthetic Declaration*, was printed on bright pink paper and posted around the capital city of Mexico for all to see.

The syndicate's *Declaration* called for a new art, rooted in Mexican Indian traditions, that would educate the people. The artists decided that the mural was the perfect vehicle for their new art—the poor, after all, could not afford to buy paintings, whereas the murals would be available to all.[5] Orozco later downplayed the syndicate's political orientation, however, maintaining that he joined the syndicate not out of any political beliefs but because membership gave him the opportunity to paint.[6]

The syndicate established a publication called *El Machete*, which quickly became the official newspaper of the Mexican Communist party. Orozco signed on

Orozco overcame his shyness to win the heart of Margarita Valladares. He often wrote her love letters to express the way he felt.

as a political artist in 1922. Because the weekly newspaper published so many antigovernment pieces, it was often suppressed by officials. For this reason, Orozco submitted many of his cartoons unsigned.

Art in Mexico took a turn for the better when Alvaro Obregón became president on December 1, 1920. He named José Vasconcelos as the secretary of education and made available to him an unusually large amount of funds to promote culture and education. Vasconcelos embarked upon establishing a system of education that would be made available to all. He also initiated a cultural program that would capitalize on Mexico's own artistic traditions in a manner similar to what the syndicate was calling for.

In the spring of 1923, Orozco and six other artists received a commission that would change the course of art in Mexico forever. During this time, Vasconcelos embarked upon an ambitious project. He envisioned a series of public murals that would inform, educate, and instill pride in Mexico's history and traditions. This period is also called the Mexican Mural Renaissance. Renaissance means "rebirth," and this term is appropriate because muralismo (the mural painting movement) had its roots in ancient Mayan and Aztec art. Many of the sixteenth-century monasteries of the Spanish colonial period were also decorated with murals. Artists from all over the world came to Mexico to see the art as it was being created.

Early on, the movement was associated with *Los Tres Grandes* (The Big Three): Diego Rivera, David Alfaro Siqueiros, and José Clemente Orozco. Secretary of Education Vasconcelos first appointed the artists to paint murals on the walls of the National Preparatory School near the Zócalo in Mexico City. Orozco himself had attended the school twenty years earlier.

The artists were given almost complete freedom as to the themes they chose for their painting—as long as the themes were Mexican. The artists depicted revolutionary ideals such as social justice, ethnic pride, and developments in agriculture, industry, and education.

Orozco immediately began to plan the murals and draw on paper some of the detailed studies he would need to guide his painting. Unlike Rivera and Siqueiros, who had studied art abroad, Orozco's training was more limited. He recognized that he was far from being an expert on fresco painting. To learn more about the technique, he read books on the subject.[7]

Fresco painting is the same technique that Italian Renaissance artist Michelangelo used in the sixteenth century when he painted the ceiling of the Sistine Chapel. *Fresco* means "fresh" in Italian and refers to the application of watercolor paint to freshly laid plaster on a wall. Plaster dries in less than a day, so only the area that can be painted in that day's work is plastered each day. Because the artist paints directly onto wet plaster, the color penetrates the wall. As the plaster hardens, the painting becomes part of the wall itself.

While mural painters are working, they are in a race against the clock each day because once the plaster dries, it is not possible to add or change any of the paint. Therefore, it is absolutely necessary that all the materials be prepared and ready to go beforehand. Because of its demanding nature, art historian E. M. Benson considers mural painting to be "unquestionably the most exacting and difficult of visual arts."[8]

The mural artist also has to have a fairly detailed idea of what will be painted. Before the artist mounts the scaffolding, sketches must be made to guide the painting. In the case of Orozco, he first thought about the building in which the mural would be painted. Then, he roughly drew the entire composition on paper, taking into consideration the wall space. Orozco then drew each figure thoroughly in detailed drawings, which then became final "cartoons." He then made a few full-size drawings that would guide him as he traced the main figures onto the wet plaster with the end of his brush or drew his designs in red color on the prepared mural surface.

Because Orozco had the use of only one hand, his assistants would prepare the walls and mix the colors under the artist's careful supervision. Orozco, however, did all his own painting. Despite his disability, Orozco matched the one-square-meter-per-day of mural space that the other artists were completing at La Prepa in each day's work of eight to ten hours.

On July 7, 1923, Orozco began his work on the walls of the Preparatoria's main patio full time. Orozco took his job as a muralist very seriously. He felt that murals could serve as educational and inspirational sources. He once said,

> Good murals are not just ordinary paintings. They are really painted bibles, and people need them as much as they need the 'talking' kind.

*L*os *Tres Grandes* (José Clemente Orozco, Diego Rivera, and David Alfaro Siqueiros) were commissioned to paint murals with a Mexican theme on the walls of the National Preparatory School in Mexico City. Pictured is the patio of "La Prepa."

> Painting on public walls is, obviously, a great
> responsibility for the artist. But when a nation
> places its trust in him, he will learn and grow and,
> at last, make himself worthy.[9]

For some of the murals, Orozco painted giant
nudes as in *Tzontemoc* and *Maternity*. For others, he
used religious themes as in *Christ Burning His Cross*
and *The Franciscan and the Indian*. He made fun of
the rich elite and lamented the condition of the common people with his *The Rich Banquet While the
Workers Fight*. Orozco also expressed his belief that
business owners and workers are always in direct
opposition to each other.

Orozco was the only muralist who never consulted
Vasconcelos about his subject matter or sought his
advice or approval. The two enjoyed a warm friendship, openly admiring each other's work. As good
friends, they also enjoyed teasing each other. One
writer who was visiting Mexico in 1923 remembers a
trip that she made with Vasconcelos to the National
Preparatory School. Orozco was absorbed in painting
a high ceiling when Vasconcelos called up to him:
"Orozco! This is the North American *periodista* [jour-
nalist], Alma Reed. She likes your painting. I don't! It's
the worst yet. But it's your wall, hombre [man], not
mine, so go ahead!" As soon as Vasconcelos and Reed
were out of Orozco's hearing distance, Vasconcelos

assured the visitor of his great admiration for the artist and his work.[10]

Not everyone embraced Orozco's artwork, however. Art critic Salvador Novo described the painter's work in the Preparatoria as "repulsive pictures."[11] Many called his murals sacrilegious, or disrespectful of the country's devout religious beliefs. A group of upper-class women, known as the Damas Católicas (Catholic Ladies), became offended by Orozco's mural *Maternity*. The women were upset that the blond woman holding a baby, who they supposed was the Virgin Mary, was depicted unclothed. They angrily called the panel "Nude Madonna" and said it was sacrilegious. Orozco protested, saying that he had no intention of painting the Virgin Mary; he was merely painting a mother and child.[12]

Others declared that Orozco's *Christ Chopping Down His Own Cross* was blasphemous. The Damas appealed to the government and demanded that Orozco remove his murals. They could not bear, the women declared, to set tables for their charity event against such a background. Government officials did nothing, however, and Orozco did not budge, saying that "fresco painting is not a cheap stage decoration that can be moved or replaced to suit a temporary mode or individual caprice [whim]."[13]

The women then took matters into their own hands. They had Orozco's scaffoldings dismantled and hung sheets, flags, shawls, and palm fronds over Orozco's work. Orozco got back at them in the mural's next panel by drawing their features in caricature form.

Despite the negative comments, many art lovers applauded the murals. Carlos Mérida, who wrote extensively on Mexican art, hailed *Maternity* as "graceful, serene, charming, recalling the Madonnas of the Italian Renaissance."[14] Many people pointed out the similarities between Orozco's composition and Botticelli's *Birth of Venus*.

During his work at La Prepa, Orozco and Margarita Valladares continued to see each other. After a two-year courtship, they decided to marry. When Orozco first told his mother of his plans, Doña Rosa could scarcely believe it. She had assumed that because of her son's overly serious personality, he would never marry. Doña Rosa immediately called Margarita, warning her that she would have a difficult time understanding her son's moodiness. Margarita assured her that she was totally in love with Orozco and they would get along very well. The couple set the wedding date for November 23, 1923, Orozco's fortieth birthday. On the afternoon of the wedding, Margarita and her family arrived at the church to find that the groom was nowhere to be found. Orozco arrived a short time later, with his mother, explaining that Doña Rosa had fainted out of sheer astonishment that she would finally witness her son's wedding.

The couple would eventually have three children. Their first child was born on September 24, 1924, while Orozco was painting at the Preparatoria. They named their son Clemente Humberto Orozco y Valladares. During the pregnancy, Margarita posed for her husband and became one of the peasant women in Orozco's murals. Their second son, Alfredo Leonardo Orozco y Valladares, was born on June 27, 1926. Their third and last child was a daughter, Eugenia Lucrecia Orozco y Valladares, born on November 13, 1927.

The family lived in a comfortable home in Coyoacán. One of Orozco's friends, MacKinley Helm, remembers the artist as a true family man—patient, affectionate, cheerful, and always concerned with the health and happiness of his children. One New Year's Day, Helm received a letter from Orozco excusing himself from a party Helm was hosting. His son Alfredo, Orozco explained, was ill and the artist wanted to stay by his side.

Although the Orozco home was a happy one, the children soon learned that their father needed absolute silence and no interruptions while he was working. Eugenia Lucrecia remembered that her father's favorite pet was a cat—he loved its movements, its elegance, and especially that it was quiet.[15] Because of Orozco's work habits, the family never owned a radio. However, the artist enjoyed classical music and took his family to concerts where they listened to Bach, Beethoven, and Mozart.

By 1924, Orozco was enjoying critical acclaim. When compared with other contemporary artists, most art critics felt that he was the best. José Juan Tablada wrote: "It is José Clemente Orozco who holds the supremacy in modern Mexican painting."[16] Tablada praised Orozco highly, calling him the "Mexican Goya." Francisco Goya was a Spanish painter whom Orozco regarded as the founder of modern art.

The open, receptive attitude toward the muralists abruptly changed with the Mexican elections in 1924. That year Plutarco Calles became president and José Vasconcelos had to leave his position as the secretary of education. Orozco felt that he had lost his protector.

In 1924, conservative students at La Prepa rioted against some of the artists' murals. The students did not agree with the liberal politics and what they perceived as antireligious sentiments promoted in some of the panels. Armed with knives, rocks, clubs, and rotten eggs, the students defaced much of Orozco's work. Several of Siqueiros's murals were similarly scratched and mutilated. Despite the muralists' many supporters, public opinion during this politically conservative time was largely with the students.

Orozco's supposedly antichurch murals were considered the main reason for the students' protest. In response to the students' actions, Orozco began to create a series of bitter caricature murals on the second floor of the building, directly above his first ones. Within a matter of two weeks, Orozco had painted an entire series of frescoes on the second floor. In these, Orozco vented his anger and disappointment by mocking the rich, the Catholic Church, injustice, and corrupt politicians.

In August 1924, Orozco was ordered to discontinue painting at the National Preparatory School because of the student demonstrations. David Alfaro Siqueiros was also dismissed. The syndicate had disintegrated, so the trade union was not able to offer much protection to the artists. Orozco retired to his home in Coyoacán and found a quiet job in the Ministry of Education, producing lettering for government publications. During this time, he also returned to newspaper cartooning.

Fortunately, Orozco received another commission after he was ordered to stop his work at La Prepa. In 1925, Orozco accepted his first private commission. It was requested by Don Francisco Sergio Iturbe, the owner of the famous *Casa de Azulejos* (House of Tiles) in the heart of Mexico City. In 1918 the building was turned into a department store, restaurant, and soda fountain with an American theme. It quickly became one of the most popular places in Mexico City.

Iturbe was a great patron of the arts whose art collection included several original drawings by

One of the most popular places in Mexico City, the House of Tiles was a combination department store and restaurant with an American theme.

Michelangelo. One day, when he was visiting the National Preparatory School, he saw one of Orozco's unfinished frescoes. The discriminating art collector was genuinely impressed. He cried: "Bring me the artist! Between him and Michelangelo there is no [other] mural painter worthy of the name!"[17]

The House of Tiles was a favorite meeting place for both locals and tourists. Since Orozco considered himself a public painter, he was especially proud that although the building was privately owned, the mural would be accessible to the general public. He titled his piece *Omnisciencia* and painted it on the main staircase. The center of the mural features a powerful female nude figure representing Grace; she looks up, smiling into a sunbeam. On either side of her are a man and a woman, the former symbolizing Force and the latter, Intelligence. The figures at either side are held back by horizontally placed arms signifying the importance of keeping force and reason in check so that humans may receive inspiration. When fellow artist Jean Charlot saw Orozco's finished composition, he sighed contentedly and wrote that here was the most beautiful wall ever painted in America."[18]

During the lull after he stopped his work at La Prepa, Orozco received a government commission to decorate the Industrial School at Orizaba. There he created a fresco called *Social Revolution* that depicted many of the bloody scenes he had witnessed during

49

Orozco's mural for the the main staircase of the House of Tiles is thought to be the most beautiful wall ever painted in the Americas.

the Mexican Revolution. Images of men with guns and knives, exhausted soldiers, and brave *soldaderas* (women soldiers) create a bitter, pessimistic mood. The last panel, however, offers some hope: The revolutionary soldiers are shown building a new society. Orozco was completing the fresco at Orizaba when he received word in early 1926 that he could resume his work at La Prepa.

Orozco's friend Anita Brenner described him as "mad with joy" on hearing the news that he would resume his work.[19] Dr. Alfonso Pruneda, the director of La Prepa, had fought so that Orozco was able to return and finish the murals already begun on the third floor and on the stairways. Thousands of Mexican and foreign art lovers had also petitioned on Orozco's behalf, sending letters urging the artist's reappointment. Orozco would also be able to restore the first and second floors that had been defaced by the students.

When Orozco surveyed the substantial damage done to the murals, his heart sank. It seems that every time a student scratched a phrase or profanity on the murals, the strict janitor of the school would come behind them with a sharp blade and remove a chunk of wall in order to remove the offensive graffiti. During Orozco's two-year absence, the murals became pockmarked with countless neat white rectangles in addition to the students' knife gashes. The artist had to tear down the panels on the ground floor altogether because of their ruined state.

When he resumed his work at La Prepa, Orozco elected to elaborate on the revolution theme that he had started at Orizaba. Paintings such as *The Destruction of the Old Order* and *The Mother's Farewell* chronicled his memories of the civil war. One of his most praised works was *Cortés and Malinche*, painted high up on a vault. The European conqueror and his Aztec servant and lover are seated, clasping hands, symbolizing the joining of the Spanish and Indian cultures. Malinche was a slave who learned Spanish and served as interpreter between the conquistador and the native peoples. Cortés later married her and the couple had a son. Dr. Pruneda was very pleased with Orozco's work, calling the third-floor works "frescoes of rare beauty and great social significance."[20]

Orozco was paid a modest five hundred pesos per month and was given an assistant to help him with the project. It was a very difficult time for Orozco because the salary was well below his family's standard of living and there was the constant threat that the project could be terminated at any moment. Although the student riots had died down, Orozco was still the object of many student pranks.

Several of Orozco's friends were concerned about the artist's growing depression and critical financial situation. They were sure that Orozco was too proud to accept money from them, so two of his friends, Manuel Rodríguez Lozano and Anita Brenner, came up with a plan. In a letter to a friend, Brenner described their scheme:

> I suggested we invent a mythical *gringo* [a man from the United States] who was writing a book about the Revolution, and who wanted illustrations. It was necessary to invent him, naturally, because we were afraid Orozco would not have taken the money from me, even in exchange for work.[21]

Lozano and Brenner told Orozco that the gringo wanted to buy six black-and-white illustrations and had left money for their purchase. In the end, Orozco completed many more drawings than just the six that were called for. The series amounted to over thirty, made up of the artist's experiences and emotions that he felt ten years earlier while traveling with Carranza's forces. Even though Orozco had created many political cartoons for *La Vanguardia* and other newspapers at the time, the artist had kept the cruelest images he had witnessed in his heart for over a decade.

Informally, Orozco called the black-and-white drawings *Los Horrores de la Revolución (The Horrors of the Revolution)*. When fellow artist and art critic Jean Charlot noted the similarities between Orozco's drawings and Goya's war etchings, Orozco replied in

Many of Orozco's murals at La Prepa had been irreparably defaced by students.

the soft voice he reserved to express anger: "I am not Goya. Goya is only a painter."[22]

Later, Charlot was left with the task of getting some of the *Horrors* drawings out of the country and into New York. Because of Orozco's earlier difficulty with United States Customs, there was concern that the drawings could be seized at the border. Charlot avoided the problem by cleverly mixing Orozco's revolutionary drawings with Charlot's own milder art. All passed Customs unquestioned. They later were shown as part of several exhibitions in New York.

In Mexico, sentiment had decidedly turned against the artists. Orozco realized that by the time he had completed the Preparatoria murals, the political and artistic tide had changed. In August 1926, he shared some newspaper clippings with a friend in which he was called hateful names: unformed, frustrated, short-sighted, and untalented. The artist admitted that if he continued to work in Mexico, he would have to "live dangerously" and be prepared to defend himself and his work from physical violence.

In 1927, Orozco decided to leave Mexico and go to New York. Even though it was difficult for him to leave his family, he felt that it was his only hope for developing his career as an artist. Orozco called upon Genaro Estrada, the secretary of foreign relations, for funds to help cover part of the transportation costs and a three-month stay. Orozco's request was granted. On December 11, with only an overnight bag as luggage, Orozco boarded the train at the Colonia railroad station. Orozco's friend Jean Charlot was the only person to see him off. Although Charlot says that Orozco left Mexico an embittered man, under Orozco's melancholy there was cautious optimism.[23] Perhaps in New York City, his luck would change.

EL NORTE

When Orozco arrived in New York in December 1927, he and other Mexican muralists were already well known in the United States. North American artists regarded the Mexicans as political and cultural heroes who were offering an artistic alternative to the isolation that North American artists felt in their own society. United States artists were inspired by the new possibilities of getting society to appreciate art. The political content, sheer size, and public display of the Mexican murals provided exciting possibilities.

Despite having his work known by fellow artists in the United States, Orozco spent his first six months in

New York in obscurity. It was a depressing and lonely time for Orozco since he had no friends, limited English ability, and a very modest budget. Since he had no contacts or patrons in New York, the three-month grant he was given by the Mexican government dwindled quickly.

Orozco lived in a simple basement studio apartment with poor lighting. It consisted of only one room and included only the most basic furniture—a bed, a drawing board, and an easel. The only human warmth was provided by his collection of family photographs that were placed around the room. At least once a week he wrote a letter to his family letting them know how he was doing.

The artist tried to contact art dealers and visit galleries, but most were not interested in his work. Orozco invited one of the best-known art buyers in New York to his studio apartment to see his drawings and paintings from the *House of Tears* and *Horrors of the Revolution* series. The dealer was impressed with Orozco's work but horrified by the subject matter. He explained to the Mexican artist that such cheerless topics would not be well received by the American public.[1] The dealer left without buying a single piece.

Orozco also tried to find employment as a political cartoonist for American magazines and newspapers. He got an interview with an editor at *The New York Times* and took along several of his cartoons that had appeared in the Mexican press. These cartoons especially poked fun at the conservative, elite sectors of society. Although the editor got a good chuckle from them, he handed the caricatures back to Orozco, explaining why he would not be able to hire the artist: "They're too good Mr. Orozco, too painfully true. You see, we'd lose circulation if we published them, because so many of our subscribers would recognize themselves."[2]

During this time Orozco painted his interpretation of his new surroundings in somber, dark pieces. For about a year, he turned away from revolutionary and Mexican themes, choosing instead to capture on canvas what he was seeing and experiencing in New York. Letters that he wrote to his wife, Margarita, and to friends in Mexico revealed isolation and sadness.

In the summer of 1928 Orozco's mood and outlook changed. He became reacquainted with Alma Reed, the journalist he had met briefly years before in Mexico City. Reed and her friend Eva Sikelianos had established "The Ashram," a salon that served as a gathering place for intellectuals and artists with the purpose of promoting Greek culture, world peace, and international harmony. They hosted lectures, poetry readings, and exhibitions of popular art. Poets, dancers, philosophers, scientists, writers, and artists from many different cultures were attracted to the Ashram. Orozco was enchanted by the elegant surroundings and enjoyed talking about the human condition over preserved orange blossoms and rose-flavored Turkish coffee.[3]

Reed and Sikelianos immediately recognized the artist's unusual talent. They were so enchanted by Orozco's art that they set out to exhibit it in their salon. They also realized that Orozco's tiny, poorly lit apartment was not a suitable place for the artist to work. Orozco was given a corner in a rear room of the Ashram to create his works of art. The spot soon became known as "Orozco's corner" to all who visited.

When he was not painting, Orozco explored the multicultural neighborhoods of New York City. Orozco was fascinated by the nightlife of Harlem, the plays at the Yiddish Theatre, the street life of Little Italy, and the wonderful restaurants in Chinatown where he learned to eat chop suey with chopsticks. He also visited Greenwich Village and Coney Island where he was amazed by the sheer number of beachgoers and extravagant side shows.

Orozco was awed by the many tall buildings in New York City. He told his friend Alma Reed, "You see, I am a public painter. For public painting one needs walls—big walls. Here you have such fine walls—such *pretty* walls!"[4] Reed had become so impressed and enchanted with Orozco's work that she soon became his agent and began to arrange the sale of his work and to obtain mural commissions for him. When Orozco's resources were dwindling, Reed even took him to the optometrist and paid the fifty-dollar fee.[5]

During the time Orozco lived in New York, he often received letters from his wife and mother. Margarita kept him informed of the children's antics and sent photos. Orozco remained close to his mother, and he was filled with great happiness when he received one of her letters. On one of Orozco's birthdays, his mother sent him a silk painting she had created that featured a beautiful house with palm trees and an arched entrance. The caption read: "My son's ideal studio." Orozco treasured the gift and vowed to one day construct a studio just as his mother envisioned.

In October 1928, Orozco had the opportunity to exhibit some of his drawings in New York City. At a group exhibition at the Art Center, twenty-two of his sketches, primarily of the Mexican Revolution, were shown alongside the works of six French artists, including Henri Matisse. Orozco was not happy with the show, complaining that the lighting was bad and that the largest pictures, none of which were his, received the most prominent display. Additionally, in order to fit one of Orozco's paintings into an old frame that was too small, the Art Center cut the work, ruining the piece's composition. In a letter to his friend Jean Charlot, Orozco concluded that the Art Center show was "a total, absolute, and definite failure."[6]

In the autumn of 1928 Orozco met Sarojini Naidu, an Indian poet and politician who was the first woman president of the Indian National Congress as well as the mayor of Bombay. She was the first woman to be elected a mayor in India. In her homeland, Naidu was a disciple of Mahatma Gandhi and worked with him in the resistance movement against British colonial rule. Naidu was especially touched by the plight of the Mexican peasant as depicted in Orozco's art, likening it to that of the poor in her native country. Orozco enjoyed his association with Naidu, warmly recollecting her elegance, poetry recitals, and conversation.[7] Some art historians feel that it was precisely after Orozco began his friendship with Naidu that his art took on a different tone. His work began to express his concern over the troubled condition of not just the Mexicans but also most of the world's people.

Orozco continued to draw on his memories of the Mexican Revolution to produce melancholy drawings in a series he called *Mexico in Revolution*, a continuation of *Horrors of the Revolution*. In October 1928, a one-man show of this series was held. Orozco was pleased with the show and wrote about the "great and magnificent results" in a letter to a friend.[8] The exhibition was well attended, and Orozco's works were properly lit and displayed.

The 1928 Christmas season was a sad one for Orozco, who was far away from his home and family.

During this time he created a small, tender oil painting called *Enseñanza* (*Teaching*). Orozco's friend Alma Reed believed that the inclusion of two young children, which was not a typical subject for the artist, was evidence of his longing to be reunited with his family.

Orozco returned to Mexico to see his family that summer. It had been a year and a half since he had seen his wife and children. Reed accompanied the artist to Pennsylvania Station and remembers the farewell:

> He checked his five shining new leather suitcases, bulging with gifts for Margarita and the children, for every member of his family, and for many of his Mexican friends. He wore a new tweed suit and carried a new topcoat. In his pocket was a new billfold containing an ample supply of crisp greenbacks [bills] which he had withdrawn the day before from his account at the Bowery Savings Bank.[9]

By all accounts, Orozco's stay in Mexico was an enjoyable one—spending time with his family, getting reacquainted with old friends, and even receiving luncheon invitations from some of the Damas Católicas who had earlier rejected his murals at La Prepa.

That summer, Reed established the Delphic Studios in New York City. The new, larger salon would serve as a center for the cultural activities of the Ashram and as an art gallery. Before Orozco returned to Mexico, he had designed much of the studio's decor.

When Orozco returned to New York in early September, he was happily surprised that his designs had been faithfully transferred from paper to reality. Soon the studio was formally inaugurated with an Orozco exhibition. Sales of works by Orozco and other artists were a daily occurrence at the gallery. The artist was very pleased with the attention his work received. He wrote to his wife: "My name and reputation are now firmly established. Without the Delphic Studios gallery, it would have been impossible!"[10]

The economic prosperity was not to last. In October 1929, the New York stock market crashed, one of a chain of events that plunged the United States and the world into an economic depression. Within a matter of weeks or even days, people lost their life's savings, businesses, or jobs. In a letter home, Orozco wrote: "The economic situation here in New York is very bad, there are many people without jobs. On every street corner there are men selling apples and lines of men who are willing to work for one dollar a week or in exchange for food."[11] The art scene was especially hard hit because paintings were considered luxury items. Sales at the Delphic Studios became increasingly infrequent.

In the midst of this dismal economic climate, Orozco was offered his first mural commission in the

United States in 1930. He was asked to paint a fresco at Pomona College in Claremont, California, near Los Angeles. Orozco was promised a fee of five thousand dollars plus room and board. Although Orozco and Reed both thought that the amount was small—considering that the wall space to be painted was very large and that the transportation and cost of materials would have to be taken from the fee—the artist agreed to the assignment.

Orozco was met at the Los Angeles railroad station by a student committee that had the unpleasant task of informing the artist that no mural fund existed for his payment. Despite his intense disappointment, Orozco had faith in the vague reassurances that the funds would be forthcoming. Besides, he reasoned, this was a golden opportunity to work on "a truly magnificent wall in the most distinguished setting to be found anywhere."[12]

Orozco was given a twenty-five-foot by thirty-five-foot recessed pointed arch on the far wall, over a fireplace, in a large student dining area in the newly constructed Frary Hall. Orozco chose Prometheus as his subject. Prometheus was the Titan who, in defiance of Zeus, stole fire from the gods and gave it as a gift to humans. As his punishment, Prometheus was chained to a mountain peak where birds pecked and tore at his liver. Orozco noticed the similarities between the defiant hero Prometheus and the role artists assume by bringing their creative gifts to the public.

Orozco completed the mural in three months. With the help of his assistant, he completed about one square yard each day. Orozco started early in the morning, had his lunch alongside the students, and worked until dark. This was no small feat for the artist, who complained in a letter to his wife that the work was often exhausting. Although he often shrugged off his disability in public, he asked Margarita for her sympathy, "Since everything, absolutely everything, I have to do [I do] with only one hand!"[13]

After the mural was finished, the college's administration presented him with a check made up of small contributions by individual professors and students. For all his efforts, Orozco felt that the fee he was paid for *Prometheus* was minuscule. The artist complained that his compensation was not even enough for his return passage to New York, which was about two hundred dollars.

Reaction to Orozco's *Prometheus* was mostly positive, although there were a few locals who protested to the selection of a foreign muralist. Some questioned why a relatively unknown Mexican artist, whose works had earlier been confiscated by border officials for being lewd, could be allowed to paint a mural of a nude man that would be seen by innocent college students.[14]

In the fall of 1930, Orozco was offered the opportunity to create a series of murals for the new building housing the New School for Social Research in New

York. Unfortunately, the newly established college did not have any funds to pay the muralist. Orozco accepted the commission, however, because of its high profile and the possibility of other commissions in the future. The only restriction placed on Orozco in choosing his theme was that he paint a contemporary subject of such great importance that in one hundred years every history book would have a chapter devoted to it.[15]

At the New School, Orozco created the most brightly colored murals he had done so far. The artist painted his ideas about the social and political changes that were currently happening in India, the Soviet Union, and Mexico. His goal was to emphasize the common humanity that all people share and their resistance to colonization. The works had titles like *Table of Brotherhood*, *The Universal Family*, and *The Strike*. In these murals Orozco featured portraits of people he admired: Vladimir Lenin; Mahatma Gandhi; and Felipe Carrillo Puerto, a popular governor from Mexico's Yucatán peninsula who was assassinated.

Struggle in the Occident was the most controversial of the New School murals. The mural is divided into two sections with the Russian Revolution on the right, and the Mexican Revolution on the left. The Russian Revolution is depicted by a commanding portrait of Lenin placed above troops brandishing their shiny bayonets, winter hoods covering their faces. To give the soldiers' bayonets their quality of murderous reality,

Orozco's murals for the New School for Social Research express his ideas about the social and political changes that were then happening in India, Mexico, and the Soviet Union. Here, the artist poses in front of the mural *Table of Brotherhood*.

Orozco used eleven different shades of white to get the gleam exactly right.[16] On the far right is a line of men symbolizing the many ethnicities that composed the Soviet Union: an Armenian, a man from India, a man of African descent, and a man from the Soviet state of Georgia who happens to be Joseph Stalin.

Carrillo Puerto's portrait is placed over a gathering of Maya Indians sitting in a semicircle. A group of blue figures in the center of the gathering form a pyramid, which is echoed above in the form of an actual pyramid, Chichén Itzá, which was the ancient capital of the Mayas in the Yucatán. The gentle portrayal of the Mexicans stands in sharp contrast to the regimented Soviet troops. In this and other murals, Orozco would suggest that the Mexican notion of reform was more worthy than the Russian version of revolution.[17]

Some of the New School's benefactors became upset when they realized that the person presiding over the gathering in *Table of Brotherhood* was an African-American man flanked by a Jew and a Mexican Indian. (Orozco believed that there could be no lasting peace in the world unless people from all cultures and countries collaborated on equal terms.)[18] The school's patrons were also upset by the portrait of the Soviet leader, Vladimir Lenin. Orozco was dismayed when these financial supporters withdrew their donations, an especially hard blow for an educational institution dependent on private contributions. The artist noted, however, that the controversy also attracted many liberal-minded individuals who pledged financial support of their own. Many of these people believed that part of art's role in modern society was to stimulate discussion and to encourage people to think about the most important issues of the day.[19]

The publicity generated by the New School murals added to Orozco's growing reputation. In the United States and abroad, the artist's work was becoming well known and admired. An exhibition of Mexican art toured throughout the major art museums in the United States and further familiarized the American public with the Mexican painter's work.

In 1931, Orozco completed an easel painting called *Zapata Entering a Peasant's Hut.* Emiliano Zapata was a peasant leader from Morelos, a southern state near Mexico City. During the Mexican Revolution, he organized an army of peasants to combat government corruption and restore land to farmers. Although Zapata was hated by the rich and powerful, to many Mexicans he became a symbol of freedom and justice. Even after the new government led by Venustiano Carranza took control, Zapata and his army continued to insist on the peasants' right to land. Zapata's popularity proved too threatening to the new government. In 1919, Carranza and the military had Emiliano Zapata murdered.

Struggle in the East was the first public monument created in honor of Mahatma Gandhi in the United States.

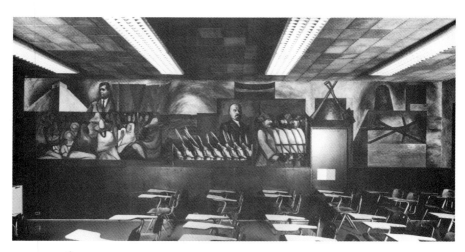

Struggle in the Occident depicts both the Russian Revolution and the Mexican Revolution.

Orozco used his usual palette of somber earth tones but also included a strong red and black. Zapata, standing over the peasants, is framed by a bright blue sky. Rather than de-emphasizing the military angle, Orozco made sure to include symbols of violence and death: a bandolier of bullets, a knife, and a bayonet that slices through the air and comes dangerously close to Zapata's eye. The painting is filled with the diagonal lines that were becoming characteristic of Orozco's work. Art critic Justino Fernández felt that the piece was "one of the most important paintings of the 20th century."[20]

Orozco soon received a private commission to create several large canvases. With this commission of twenty-five hundred dollars the artist was able to send for his wife and children. They arrived in New York in April 1931, after Orozco had secured two large apartments—one to serve as the family living quarters, the other as his studio. Since Margarita had studied English in school, she had no language difficulty.

Happy to be reunited with his family, Orozco now embarked on a very productive period of oil painting that gained him more commissions and prominence. His name soon reached a New England college that was in need of someone to demonstrate the ancient art of fresco.

THE ARTIST IN
NEW ENGLAND

By 1932, José Clemente Orozco had developed a good reputation throughout the United States. In May, Orozco was invited to Dartmouth College in Hanover, New Hampshire. He had received word of a visiting professor position at Dartmouth offered by the college's president, Ernest Martin Hopkins. The wealthy and influential businessman Nelson Rockefeller, a Dartmouth graduate, personally recommended Orozco for the job and provided the funds for the professorship. The Rockefeller family was a great patron of Mexican art in the United States and had established a special teaching fund at the college.

As an artist in residence in the Department of Art, Orozco's job was to demonstrate fresco painting to art students by teaching and demonstrating. This was an innovative plan for the time since few colleges were studying the work of living artists. The art history professors wanted to involve their students more closely in the creative process by having them observe Orozco as he worked.

At first, Orozco demonstrated his method on a fifty-foot space in the corridor connecting the Baker Library with the Carpenter Art Building. On the first morning of Orozco's assignment, the artist arrived to find students and professors crowded into the hallway. The plaster surface had already been prepared by the mason entrusted to the job. Nervously, Orozco climbed onto the scaffolding and picked up a brush with his one hand. He began by applying some blue background color to the upper right corner. To the artist's great embarrassment, the water-based color would not take. Even though he had used this same technique many times before, the paint just dripped down the wall no matter how carefully he tried to apply it. Later, when Orozco questioned the mason, he found out that his well-meaning assistant had mixed a special formula of plaster in honor of the visiting muralist. "There can't be anything wrong with the plaster," said the mason. "It's guaranteed to be waterproof!"[1]

After working out a usable formula with the mason, Orozco began to create his fresco. Using his "lecturing with a brush" method, Orozco executed a small fresco called *Man Released from the Mechanistic*. By showing an optimistic, wide-eyed young man rising out of a pile of broken machine parts, Orozco expressed his vision of humans' escape from the destruction that machines and modern technology can cause.

In June 1932, just a month after he arrived at Dartmouth, Orozco announced that he had found the perfect space for the execution of a mural project he had dreamed of for a long time. The newly constructed Baker Library, with an impressive collection of books in Spanish, had a reserve room in the basement. There Orozco discovered three thousand square feet of long, straight wall space that would be perfect for his project. The artist hoped to execute what would be the greatest work of his career: the history of American civilization.[2]

On hearing of his plans, the college, using Rockefeller's donation, immediately offered him a regular faculty position so that he could realize his dream. Orozco would be paid seventy-seven hundred dollars in wages plus additional money for painting materials and expenses.[3] Dartmouth agreed to give the artist the freedom to execute the mural as he wished—the only restriction was that worthy students would be allowed to watch and work with him. Orozco agreed to teach classes beginning in the fall semester, supervise students, and complete his project. Orozco rented a house near campus and arranged for his wife and children to join him.

That summer, Orozco went on a very special trip. The fifty-year-old artist visited Europe for his first and only time. His stay there was brief—just three months—but during that time he was able to see many of the great artists that he had studied and copied in school. He traveled to Spain, England, France, and Italy and visited many museums, churches, and architectural monuments while there. It was a special treat for him to see firsthand the frescoes of the masters that he had only heard or read about: Leonardo da Vinci's *Last Supper*, Michelangelo's Sistine Chapel, and Giotto di Bondone's *Resurrection of Lazarus*.

On his return to Dartmouth, Orozco settled down to absorb the New England atmosphere with his family. He and Margarita were immediately charmed by their new surroundings and with the hospitality of the New Englanders. Margarita quickly became friends with several women and was invited to many social events.[4]

Orozco began his mural work at Dartmouth by thinking about the wall space and roughly sketching his ideas. In preparation, Orozco made about four hundred preliminary drawings. He also produced a few full-size drawings to guide his painting. As he painted his vision of the development of civilization in the

Baker Library, Dartmouth College
Hanover, New Hampshire, 1932–1934

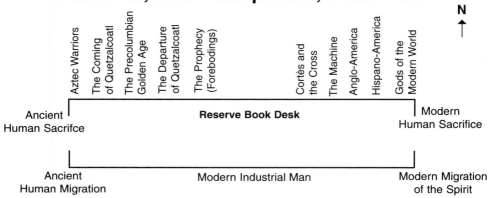

N ↑

Aztec Warriors
The Coming of Quetzalcoatl
The Precolumbian Golden Age
The Departure of Quetzalcoatl
The Prophecy (Forebodings)

Cortés and the Cross
The Machine
Anglo-America
Hispano-America
Gods of the Modern World

Ancient Human Sacrifce

Reserve Book Desk

Modern Human Sacrifice

Ancient Human Migration

Modern Industrial Man

Modern Migration of the Spirit

The New School for Social Research,
New York, 1930

↓ **N**

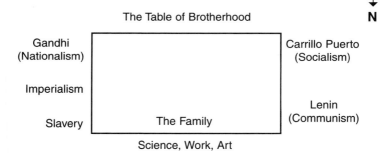

The Table of Brotherhood

Gandhi (Nationalism)

Carrillo Puerto (Socialism)

Imperialism

Slavery

The Family

Lenin (Communism)

Science, Work, Art

In Dartmouth's Baker Library, Orozco painted his depiction of the entire history of American civilization. His murals at the New School for Social Research dealt with historic changes throughout the whole world.

Americas, Orozco chose to tell much of the story
through themes from ancient Mexican culture. In the
end, Orozco covered about twenty-two hundred
square feet of wall in the Baker Library with twenty-
four panels. He usually finished only a few square feet
a day. Some days he spent the entire time painting
details on a face or hands.

The large expanse of wall in the Baker Library is
virtually uninterrupted with the exception of a few air
vents. When Orozco realized that the metallic grid of a
vent could not be removed from the wall, he said,
"Very well. My problem is to work within the architectural frame. I will paint this panel in such a manner that
if you take the ventilator away you will spoil my composition." And with expert composure, he did.[5]

Although the mural wraps around four walls of the
room, Orozco separated his epic mural, thematically
and architecturally, into two parts: *The Coming of
Quetzalcoatl* (part 1) and *The Return of Quetzalcoatl*
(part 2). Part 1 depicts life in North and South America
before the arrival of the Europeans. Part 2 portrays the
arrival of the European explorers, beginning with
Hernando Cortés, life since the subsequent conquest
of the New World, and a vision for the future.

The Coming of Quetzalcoatl is based on the legend
of the plumed serpent creator god, Quetzalcoatl. The
great divine being arrives among the peoples of pre-
Columbian America, who are shown practicing

witchcraft and human sacrifice. Quetzalcoatl introduces them to industry, art, and science and offers them a new, more civilized way of life. After a period of peace and prosperity, however, certain priests wanted to return to the old ways and reject Quetzalcoatl's offerings. The god leaves on a raft of serpents, warning them that he will return one day to destroy those who have rejected his teachings and gifts and to set up a new civilization.

In *The Return of Quetzalcoatl*, Cortés arrives holding a sword and followed by a monk bearing a cross, symbolizing the arrival of the Catholic Church. The Spanish conquistador's coming marks a bloody beginning for the new civilization. Orozco's murals suggest that the superior military technology of the Europeans developed into a society governed by machinery, which dehumanizes people. Orozco also shows his hatred of military power by the anonymous corpse of a soldier in another panel called *Modern Human Sacrifice.*

A panel called *Anglo-America* reflects Orozco's admiration of some aspects of North American culture. In *Anglo-America* a schoolteacher is surrounded by her students. In the background are the symbols of middle America: an orderly town meeting, a house, barns, and wheat fields. A brilliant, ultramarine blue sky is behind it all. Some art critics felt that *Anglo-America*'s tone was far from positive, however. Writer Bernard S.

Orozco was as devoted to his family as he was to his art. He often enjoyed a quiet game of cards with his wife, Margarita, and their daughter, Eugenia Lucrecia.

Myers, for example, considered the schoolteacher to be "blank-faced and unpleasant-looking surrounded by equally uninspiring youngsters."[6] It is this very ambiguity that makes so many of Orozco's works open to interpretation by the viewer.

The most controversial of all the panels was probably *Gods of the Modern World*, which features the birthing scene of a skeleton dressed in a college cap and gown. Orozco drew on the early influence of the printmaker Posada and used *calaveras* to depict the characters. The female skeleton is lying on a bed of ragged books. The skeletal baby she delivers is still-born, but identical to the academic gods in the background who turn their backs to the problems of the modern world. With this scene, Orozco conveyed quite clearly that he was not convinced that academic training is always very effective.[7] This mural is, in fact, criticizing the glorification of useless knowledge that has no relevance to modern society.

His final panel, *Modern Industrial Man*, is a utopian view of the future in which machines serve humankind rather than destroy them. With the new leisure time that machinery has given him, a worker is shown reclining, reading a book.

When Orozco finished the series, an art critic proclaimed that not only had the muralist "produced probably the most impressive mural in North America, [but] he had added a new course to the curriculum."[8] The artist himself pointed out that in a large mural project such as the one at Dartmouth, individual panels could not be understood on their own. The artist felt that the entire composition had to be regarded as a whole.

Almost immediately, there was a strong reaction to Orozco's work from some art critics and from the public. Some called the frescoes "hideous" and "grisly."[9] Others declared that such themes and artistic techniques did not belong to the New England tradition, arguing

The work of José Guadalupe Posada, known as the father of Mexican printmaking, influenced Orozco's *Gods of the Modern World* panel in Dartmouth's Baker Library. Posada, far right, stands in front of his shop in Mexico City.

that local artists should have been commissioned instead. Some Unites States artists also objected to the selection of a Mexican artist for a project at the height of the Depression. Dartmouth president Hopkins was pressured to destroy the murals. He stood firm, however, and the work survived unharmed.

Despite the strong outcry, many more people supported Orozco. One critic wrote that the "spiritual vitality of genuine New England is better embodied in Orozco's murals than in any amount of local history tamely recorded by local artists."[10] Years later, one of the Dartmouth art history professors commented, "We knew we'd get a good painting. We had no idea we'd get a masterpiece."[11]

Each day that summer, about two hundred and fifty people visited the Baker Library to catch a glimpse of the Orozco murals. President Hopkins noted that almost everyone who went to the Maine coast for their summer vacation drove there by way of Hanover to see the murals.[12] Groups of artists also organized trips to the college to see and study the murals.

As productive and rewarding as his time had been in the United States, though, it was now time for Orozco to return to his home in Mexico.

CHAPTER SEVEN

BACK HOME

Orozco had been gone from his homeland seven years when he returned with his family in 1934. He returned to a hero's welcome and a wonderful opportunity. The magnificent white marble opera house that had been built under President Díaz was going to be inaugurated in September of that year as the *Palacio de Bellas Artes* (Palace of Fine Arts).

Officials wanted the interior walls to be decorated with Mexican art. Diego Rivera had been given the east wall on the second floor of the lobby and was already at work creating his *Man at the Crossroads*. Orozco was offered a commission to paint the opposite west wall, which he immediately accepted. For Orozco, it must have seemed like sweet irony that just a few years before, his art had provoked harsh criticism.

Orozco's piece, called *Catharsis*, symbolized the abuses and brutality that destroy humanity and society. The evil forces of the world are depicted by military men carrying rifles, while the degenerate pleasures of the rich are symbolized by seminude, reclining women. Humanity's constant struggle for a more equal and fair world is portrayed by a nude torso of a man fighting the corruption. On the right side of the mural is Orozco's by-now familiar theme of industry imprisoning and enslaving humans.

In 1935 Orozco's mother, Rosa, died of a heart attack. A few weeks earlier Margarita, who took care of her, had noticed that the elderly woman lost all appetite. Despite her son's or daughter-in-law's pleas, Rosa refused to eat. Finally, on the morning of October 13, her heart stopped. She was eighty-six years old. Because his mother had been such a central part of his life, Orozco was filled with an enormous sadness.

Orozco was still grieving the loss of his beloved mother when he received word of a government commission in Guadalajara, Mexico. In 1936 he was asked by Jalisco governor C. Everardo Topete to create frescoes for the State University of Jalisco in Guadalajara. Orozco's most impressive mural was done in the cupola, or dome, of the auditorium. Orozco called his

O rozco's mural for the Palace of Fine Arts titled *Catharsis,* depicted the abuses and brutality that destroy society.

fresco *Creative Man.* On it he depicted four great characters in human history: the teacher, the worker, the scientist, and the rebel. Although each of the figures maintains his individuality, they each intersect and connect with one another.

In 1937, Orozco was commissioned to create a fresco in Guadalajara's Government Palace. The Spanish-colonial palace had been built in the mid-1600s and featured a huge, winding staircase that would serve as Orozco's canvas. Orozco chose to paint his interpretation of the history that the building had witnessed in its three centuries of existence.

The mural series begins with a commanding Father Miguel Hidalgo y Costilla, the priest-leader of Mexico's revolt against Spain in the nineteenth century. In Orozco's fresco, Father Hidalgo, lips parted, raises one arm with a clenched fist and carries a flaming torch in the other, calling Mexico to war. The colors Orozco used—rich brown for Hidalgo's skin, snowy white for his hair, somber black for his coat, and vivid red for the blaze—provide dramatic contrasts.

In 1938, the fifty-five-year-old Orozco began work on the chapel of Guadalajara's Hospicio de Niños Cabañas (Cabañas Orphanage). Orozco was appointed to create frescoes for the walls, roof, and cupola of the chapel at the Hospicio Cabañas, a total of twelve hundred square meters (about one thousand square feet). While the artist worked there, five hundred children lived and attended school in the Hospicio. A writer at the time noted that Orozco's painting would serve a fine purpose: to contribute to the education, understanding, and maturity of tomorrow's citizens, workers, and teachers.[1]

As in the Dartmouth murals, Orozco chose as his theme the history and development of the Americas. The most vivid fresco in the series is *Man of Fire*, painted in the cupola of the chapel. In this work humankind seems to be engulfed in, yet emerging from, an inferno. It can be interpreted as either a beginning or an ending. Many feel that the Guadalajara murals represent some of Orozco's most impressive achievements. Friend and writer Luis Cardoza y Aragón insisted that "Those who do not know Orozco at Guadalajara do not know Orozco."[2] For many art lovers, this mural perfectly illustrates Orozco's definition of art. When asked to define art, he replied simply: "Art is knowledge at the service of emotion."[3]

Orozco's artwork at the Hospicio Cabañas—which he chose to execute in vibrant oranges, reds, grays, and black—is in beautiful contrast to the chapel's cool gray stone. Some feel that because of the range of warm colors that Orozco used, this can be considered "the happiest of his works."[4] In fact, many art critics and art lovers feel that the Cabañas frescoes are Orozco's greatest accomplishment.[5] Some have compared them with Michelangelo's Sistine Chapel because of their grand style, heroism, and somber quality.[6]

In 1940, the outgoing president Lázaro Cárdenas wanted to make a gift to his native city of Jiquilpán. He offered Orozco another commission: to create murals for the Gabino Ortíz Library in Jiquilpán, Mexico. The library had been converted from a nineteenth-century chapel with long, high walls and arches.

Known sometimes as *Desastres de la Guerra* (*Disasters of War*), the murals are violent, painted in harsh black and white with only the flags painted in brilliant colors. Orozco's monochromatic technique

Orozco's assistant is shown preparing a wall for one of the artist's frescos.

had a very aggressive effect. One art critic felt that the black-and-white murals were evidence of the influence of Posada's black-and-white artistic style on the artist when he was young.[7]

While Orozco was still working on the murals in Jiquilpán, he was called to the United States by the Museum of Modern Art (MOMA) in New York. As part of its exhibition, "Twenty Centuries of Mexican Art," MOMA offered Orozco his fourth mural commission in the United States. Orozco's mural was conceived as a work in progress. He first thought about the mural on the train ride from Mexico. Then, the artist spent a month in his Manhattan hotel working on the preliminary drawings. While Orozco painted, he allowed visitors to watch the mural's development.

Orozco titled the piece *A Dive Bomber and Tank*. Dressed in overalls and wearing his thick glasses, he answered questions while he worked, explaining the complexities and difficulties of mural painting. He worked every day from eight in the morning until four or five in the afternoon. With the help of one assistant, the artist completed the work within ten days, from June 21 to June 30, 1940. Orozco enjoyed himself tremendously during this time. Viewers commented that the one-handed artist made fresco painting look so effortless, it was easy to imagine that if one had two hands one could paint automatically.[8]

Part of the reason people were so interested in the mural was that Orozco announced early on that it would be painted on six detachable, portable plaster panels that could be shown right side up or upside down, in any order, even with some panels omitted. In fact, Orozco felt that to truly understand the composition, the viewer had to contemplate it from many different angles.[9] Because they were movable, the panels could, in effect, later be sent on a traveling exhibition throughout the country. However, this plan proved to be more difficult than he imagined. The

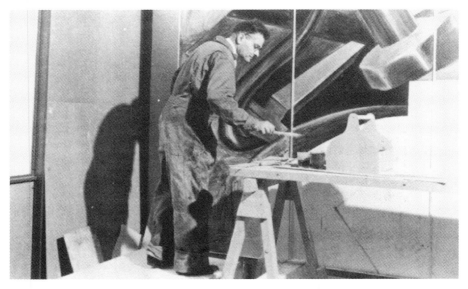

Orozco at work creating the mural *Dive Bomber and Tank* in the Museum of Modern Art in New York City.

nine- by three-foot plaster panels, set into steel frames, wound up weighing a total of one and a half tons.

The mural's title itself caused confusion. The composition is made up of tanks, machine pieces, and parts of airplanes. Within the intricate design, three masks stare out with empty eyes. Most people claimed that they could not even discern a dive bomber within the piece. (A dive bomber is a plane that was invented and developed by the U.S. Army and used by the German Air Force to bomb much of Europe.) In a letter written to a friend on June 21, 1940, Orozco described the subject matter as "something like an airplane for war or a tank, with some figures. [It will have] no meaning or symbolism except the one the spectator may think it has."[10] Orozco explained that the mural was not intended to be a realistic, detailed painting of an actual dive bomber. Instead, it was supposed to convey a sense of the power of modern warfare. He said: "That is what modern art is, the actual feeling of life around us or the mood of whatever is just happening."[11]

When the public demanded program notes to guide their viewing, Orozco became upset. He published his response, titled "Orozco 'Explains,'" in a MOMA *Bulletin*. In it, a frustrated Orozco wrote: "The public refuses TO SEE painting. They want TO HEAR painting. They don't care for the show itself, they prefer TO LISTEN to the barker outside. 'Free lectures every hour for the blind, around the Museum. This way, please.'"[12]

After finishing *Dive Bomber and Tank* for the Museum of Modern Art in New York City, the painter collected his sizable fee. He knew just what he would do with the money. Using plans that had been designed by his mother, he would build a new art studio in Mexico City.

A PRODUCTIVE LIFE

When Orozco returned to his homeland after completing *Dive Bomber*, he constructed a cheerful new studio for himself in the nation's capital. Using the silk painting his mother had made that depicted her vision of an ideal studio, Orozco designed a roomy studio on Ignacio Mariscal Street in Mexico City. Since Orozco painted using only natural light, he hung white cotton curtains and made sure that the studio had a northern exposure. He explained to Margarita that the light that came from the north had a clearer, bluish tinge whereas southern light had a yellowish cast he did not care for. Later, when he moved to Guadalajara, he used the same plan and constructed an even more spacious studio.

Soon after his return in January 1941, Orozco was commissioned to decorate the new Supreme Court Building that had recently been built. Never one to select an uncomplicated subject, Orozco used a palette of sickly greens and grays to criticize the often unfair justice system. Alvin Johnson, the president of the New School for Social Research in New York, had noticed that Orozco painted the past or what was destined for defeat in grays. Those things or people who held promise were painted in brighter and deeper colors.[1]

In *False Justice*, Justice is depicted as an angel coming down to Earth to strike down corruption. While he painted, Orozco had to endure the almost daily protests of lawyers and judges who felt that the artist was mocking them and their profession.[2]

By the 1940s, Orozco was not only well known throughout Mexico, but also had developed a respectful and devoted following. Much of his income was derived from painting the portraits of wealthy citizens. The admiring nation did not know much about the reclusive artist, however. There were many requests for his biography. The humble Orozco could not understand why anyone would be interested in his life. He said of his life: "There is nothing of special interest in it, no famous exploits or heroic deeds, no extraordinary or miraculous happenings. Only the uninterrupted and tremendous efforts of a Mexican painter to learn his trade and find opportunities to practice it."[3]

Between February 17 and April 8, 1942, Orozco's autobiography was published in fifteen installments in one of Mexico City's newspapers, *Excelsior*. Curiously, Orozco does not mention his beloved family anywhere in his autobiography. He was also careful not to reveal any of the difficulties he might have suffered because of his physical or financial limitations.

In the English-speaking world, Orozco's work was reaching more people as his illustrations were included in several novels. When John Steinbeck's *The Pearl* was published, it featured drawings by Orozco. The story centers around a fisherman named Kino, his wife, Juana, and their baby, Coyotito. Orozco's simple ink drawings enhance the emotions evoked by the novel.

From 1942 to 1947 Orozco worked, off and on, on murals for the Hospital de Jesús Nazareno in Mexico City. The ancient hospital had been founded by Hernando Cortés early in the 1500s and was said to be the first of its kind in the Americas. According to legend, the hospital was built in the very same place where Cortés met Montezuma for the first time.

Orozco's work was a labor of love since no government bureau commissioned the mural. He even had to construct his own scaffold to reach the fifty-foot vaulted ceiling. The color scheme the artist chose was cool—mostly grays, greens, and black—perfect for the scenes of angels and demons he envisioned.

A friend who visited Orozco while he was at work at the Jesús Hospital was amazed at the physical effort that was required to climb the tall scaffolding and paint under the difficult conditions. By that time, the painter was sixty years old and was growing frailer. The friend recalls:

> The scaffolding creaked and groaned under the strain of our ascent to the vaulting. The hazards and discomforts of the fifty-foot climb kept me gasping while Orozco, seemingly quite unshaken, lifted a bucket of brushes and colors from the end of his stump and began to draw on the dry plaster surface of one of the circular vaults. I remember protesting to the Señora de Orozco about the unwisdom of his working at such a strenuous height in the nerve-wracking altitude of Mexico City. She said she had tried to keep her husband away from the temple two or three days in the week, on one pretext or another, for she knew that he was rapidly exhausting his body. But the painter was not to be stopped by any thought for himself. He kept working in a frenzy until his money ran out.[4]

Orozco worked on the murals at first for two years, but the meager funds soon ended. Working in bits and pieces thereafter, he never fully completed the murals.

Orozco's daily life was one of work, reflection, and long walks with his wife, Margarita. He always woke

Orozco directs his assistants while at work on a mural for the National School for Teachers in Mexico City.

early, and after breakfast he would immediately go to whichever building he was currently painting. Orozco painted until one in the afternoon at which point he ate a light lunch that enabled him to continue working until the late afternoon. The artist then returned home and had a more substantial meal with his family. Each evening Orozco went for a long walk; it was his favorite form of exercise. Margarita remembered that her husband kept such a brisk pace that whoever accompanied him had a very difficult time keeping up. At night Orozco read for about two hours.[5]

In 1947 Orozco was awarded Mexico's National Prize in the Arts and Sciences. The prestigious national prize is bestowed every five years on the citizen who has contributed the most to Mexican society in culture, science, literature, or art. In conjunction with the prize, Orozco had a 1947 exhibition in the Palace of Fine Arts in Mexico City. The showing included early works from his experiences in brothels and battlefields as well as oil paintings done later in life.

That same year, he was asked to create a huge fresco for the outdoor theater and stadium of the Escuela Normal Nacional (National School for Teachers) in Mexico City. Despite his considerable mural experience, Orozco had never worked on an outdoor mural. His biggest challenge was to find paint and colors that would be weatherproof. The artist realized that if he created the mural using his usual fresco technique, the work might not be very durable. He finally settled on a very unusual selection: automobile spray paint. After consulting a chemist-technician, Orozco developed a formula for the paint. By mixing ethyl silicate (a type of paint), alcohol, water, and hydrochloric acid, he created a compound that held the pigment until it was applied. Once the alcohol evaporated, the resulting gel would dry quickly and preserve the color on the concrete surface.

Once he solved the technical problems, Orozco began *National Allegory* in November 1947. Clearly, Orozoco's technique had to be modified to suit the gigantic outdoor scale of this new project. To outline the figures he would paint, he etched the lines into the dry concrete with a drill. He also had to work around a sixteenth-century doorway that was placed in the wall.

Another thing to consider was the theme. The easy thing to do would be to paint a collage of images from a teacher's life. But Orozco understood that such a painting would compete with speakers or actors on the stage.[6] Because the wall would be a backdrop to the outdoor theater, Orozco decided to paint an abstract composition that would not detract too much from the activity on stage. He chose the theme of Mexico's struggle to improve itself through education. Using the body of a serpent, representing Mexico, embedded in a series of triangles, circles, and spirals, Orozco was able to portray the upward reach of his homeland. Art lovers have taken it to mean that by using technology, mathematics, and other sciences, Mexico will reach its full development in the future. With the aid of assisting artists, Orozco completed *National Allegory* in April 1948.

At the end of that year Orozco undertook yet another project. He accepted the commission to decorate the concert hall of the newly constructed National Conservatory of Music. It was to be another outdoor mural—the stage wall of an open-air auditorium. The project was unique because for the first time in his life, Orozco would create an artistic combination of painting and sculpture. Although he had never sculpted before, Orozco was excited by the prospect.[7]

Orozco had barely begun the work when he was called away on another commission to the Government Palace in Guadalajara, where he had painted Father Hidalgo on the staircase. Once there, Orozco was given the dome of the Senate Chamber to paint. The artist decided to return to the Hidalgo theme, this time concentrating on the leader-priest's efforts to end slavery. Father Hidalgo signed the decree in 1810 that abolished slavery for the first time in the Americas. At the base of the fresco are three chained slaves with whip marks on their backs. Hidalgo is in the center, writing the word *Libertad* (Liberty) on a banner.

That month, the artist returned to Mexico City to another project conceived by architect Mario Pani. Pani had designed and constructed the Miguel Alemán housing complex in the southern part of the city to benefit middle- and low-income families. The architect wanted Orozco to create a mural for a curving garden wall, where Pani envisioned happy tenants having their spirits uplifted as they took their evening strolls.[8] In preparation, Orozco had created a series of colored cartoons that would guide him in his painting. He would call the mural *Primavera (Spring)*.

Orozco's cardiologist, Ignacio Chávez, advised his patient that he should not continue working on murals. Because of some recurring bouts with bronchitis, Dr. Chávez warned, Orozco's heart was getting weaker and suggested that the artist should concentrate his efforts on the less strenuous work of easel painting. Orozco solemnly said to his wife, "I'm not going to do as the doctor says and abandon mural painting. I prefer physical death to the moral death that would be the equivalent of giving up mural painting."[9]

Orozco arrived at the Miguel Alemán apartment complex garden clutching one of his cartoons on the morning of September 6, 1949. After a few minutes of working on a reclining figure in the mural, he put down his brush and lay down in some shade on the grass. When one of his assistants asked if he was all right, the artist replied that he was fine, just very tired. After

Orozco takes a rare break during his work in the open-air theater of the National School for Teachers.

having a bit of lunch, Orozco packed up his brushes and started for home earlier than usual. When the assistant asked him why he was leaving, Orozco replied, "I am going home because I am so terribly tired. But maybe, maybe we shall see each other tomorrow."[10]

That evening, the assistant commented to his wife that he was bothered by Orozco's reply: "The maestro didn't say 'See you tomorrow,' as usual. He said 'See you *tal vez*—maybe—tomorrow.'"[11] The assistant's fears were confirmed when the artist did not show up at the project the following morning. On September 7, 1949, José Clemente Orozco died at home of a heart attack. He was sixty-five years old.

Orozco had been sleeping next to his wife, Margarita, when she was abruptly awakened by her husband's labored breathing at 6:30 A.M. She immediately called his doctor, who rushed to the house. While Margarita waited outside the room, the doctor tried in vain to revive Orozco. Dr. Chávez emerged after a while to console Margarita, saying that Orozco had died peacefully in his sleep.

As is Mexican custom, the windows of his studio were covered with dark cloth. As news of his death spread throughout the city, fellow artists and students crowded in front of Orozco's house. Friends, relatives, and government officials called on his widow, Margarita, and the three children to pay their respects.

$\mathcal{S}$ tanding left to right at Orozco's state funeral are Fernando Gamboa, Alfredo Orozco, Clemente Orozco, and Diego Rivera.

Newspapers throughout Mexico and the world published tributes to the artist and printed many of his works. Mexican art critic Justino Fernández wrote, "Orozco is dead and Mexico mourns; all through the Americas there will be grief and sorrow because his prodigious [extraordinary] hand can never again paint the truth as he alone knew how to paint it."[12]

In Mexico, the National Congress decreed two days of national mourning. When introducing the proclamation in the Cabinet, congressional representatives said: "Today we have lost the great Mexican painter

José Clemente Orozco, whose death represents the loss of one of our most sacred artistic treasures in our country."[13] Orozco's body was prepared and placed in a black-draped coffin in the Palace of Fine Arts. Against a massive display of flowers, the president and his cabinet stood in attendance. Siqueiros and Rivera stood as honor guards at his bier (the stand on which the coffin was placed) and delivered eloquent speeches lavishly praising their fallen colleague.

After the service, hundreds of schoolchildren, art students, university professors, and ordinary citizens walked in a solemn parade from the Palace of Fine Arts to the Rotunda de los Hombres Ilustres (Rotunda of the Illustrious Men) in the Civil Cemetery. The National Congress honored the artist by decreeing that his body be buried in the Rotunda, which holds the bodies of Mexico's greatest heroes.

HIS LEGACY, HIS ART

When asked to describe José Clemente Orozco, one person said: "A slight, gentle, bespectacled man with about 20 teeth, Orozco has no left hand, no hearing in his left ear, and very poor eyesight."[1] To many people who met Orozco for the first time, the artist might have looked like an invalid. Despite his physical handicaps, everyone who knew Orozco invariably spoke of his strength, his stature, and his talent. Describing a meeting that he had with Orozco toward the end of the artist's life, writer Alfred Neumeyer remembered:

. . . this incapacitated being was the same one who, year in, year out, would cover the walls of Mexican buildings with an 'orbis pictus' for his people. He seemed to me the very embodiment [symbol] of the triumph of the creative spirit over physical limitations.[2]

In a tribute published shortly after the artist's death, Justino Fernández called Orozco the "genius of America, the first great creative genius in American art, the first one to appear since America became America."[3] Mexican writer Octavio Paz agreed with that assessment, declaring, "He was a truly free man and artist, and something extraordinary for Mexico, he was not afraid to express his freedom."[4]

Orozco expressed this freedom in a number of unconventional ways. His friend, artist and writer Jean Charlot, felt that Orozco earned the description of "loner" by always seemingly going against the grain—experimenting with new techniques, choosing sensitive topics, and being fearless in his depiction of ideas that were often contrary to what others were doing.[5]

In selecting themes for his murals, Orozco was often alone. During the upheaval of the 1930s, most North and South American artists were representing technological progress as a savior for humanity. Orozco was unusual because he recognized that technology and machinery have both positive and negative sides.

Art curator Jacquelyn Baas said, "Orozco always did the hard thing. At Dartmouth, he did a panel that criticized higher education; for a Supreme Court mural in Mexico, he did a panel criticizing justice."[6] At the time, one newspaper article noted, "José Clemente Orozco seems to possess the faculty for stirring up controversy wherever he works."[7] When he finished the New School murals a writer summed up Orozco's uniqueness this way: "Orozco has always been a law unto himself, saying what he wanted to say in his own way."[8]

In his mural paintings, Orozco painted human bodies with defects, disproportions, and exaggerated features. While many people criticized the ugliness of Orozco's renditions, many more applauded his realism. When the Catholic Archbishop of Mexico, Don Luis María Martínez, was to have his portrait painted, he specifically asked for Orozco. "Orozco is an honest artist," said the archbishop, "and will not flatter me as others have done but portray me in my natural aspect."[9] Even those dearest to him were presented in truthful detail. When Orozco painted a portrait of his wife, Margarita, he included the mild cross-eyed condition from which she sometimes suffered.

Although Orozco dabbled in many art forms, the mural remained his favorite medium throughout his artistic career. He left a legacy of 116 mural panels and countless preparatory studies. Part of the reason Orozco preferred murals was that, because of their public nature, they are available to all people. Orozco also recognized that mural painting was one of the most difficult types of art to execute. "Improvement," he said, "comes only through hard discipline, and fresco is one of the most important means to that end, since it demands from the painter all his energy, all his time, and all his attention."[10] Even when Orozco created easel paintings, the works had such a sense of largeness that they seemed to be meant to occupy a panel in a mural design.

Orozco admitted that he himself was frequently unable to explain the symbolism he used in his painting. He often said that it was impossible for him to invent a title or explain the content of his works. That, the artist argued, was the function of the painting itself.[11] Sometimes, if he was pressed to title a painting, he would tell the inquirer in exasperation, "The title is 'Whatever You Like'!"

Orozco also felt that, since viewers bring to any art their own ideas and perspectives, each piece of art is subject to many interpretations. He once gave the example of a picture representing a war scene. Orozco said that one person might start thinking of murder, another of peace, another of the human body, and yet another of history. Therefore, he argued, while a painting may present an idea, it is impossible for a painting to tell a story. Only humans can do the latter.[12]

For the most part, Orozco's view of humanity and its history was pessimistic. He repeatedly expressed his loathing of oppression and corruption. The "bad guys" in Orozco's art are clearly identified: corrupt politicians, the rich, leaders of the church, and dishonest labor leaders with only their own interests at heart. These are all depicted in harsh and vivid detail. The "good guys," that is, the workers and peasants, all remain anonymous in Orozco's paintings—their faces covered, hidden, or turned away. The viewer gets the feeling that repeated cruelty has stripped the poor of their individual identity.

Many art critics feel that the main characteristic of Orozco's murals is that he painted the ugly, the negative, the bad in human beings.[13] While it is true that he often depicted the insensitivity that humans have shown one another, he was deeply concerned for the fate of humankind. Orozco once had his fortune told by Alma Reed's mother, who did readings for friends as an amusement. One day she asked the artist to cut a deck of cards and make a wish. At the end of the reading, she told him that his wish would not come true. "Ah, that is bad—very bad," Orozco exclaimed. "Why, Clemente, what was your wish?" she asked. "I wished for peace and for happiness for all humanity," he replied softly.[14]

Orozco's tombstone is at the Rotunda de los Hombres Ilustres in Mexico City.

Many of Orozco's paintings and drawings show a lot of detail in the hands. Some feel that this preoccupation had its roots in his maiming. In his later years, Orozco insisted that the loss had never been a handicap.

Like Rivera, Siqueiros, and the printmaker José Guadalupe Posada, Orozco used print and painting as a way to express the political and social condition of his time. However, unlike Rivera and Siqueiros, who were both avowed Marxists, Orozco remained noncommittal about his political beliefs and goals. Art critic Peter Yates said, "His [Orozco's] social satire may seem to wear the Communist label, but it is really Populist." Yates observed, "What Orozco has to say is still too much for us. It strikes directly at conscience: our conscience would prefer not to deal politely with any art that packs so stiff a wallop."[15]

During the 1930s, Orozco and his colleagues in the Mexican muralist movement had great impact on North American artists. The political themes and the public nature of mural art were traits that were particularly attractive to artists in the United States. During this period of economic and sociopolitical upheaval, Mexican art represented conflict and struggle on a national, even epic, scale.

Despite the support Mexican mural art enjoyed before World War II, it was rejected by later generations, who favored celebrating privacy, personal freedom, and the individual, and were suspicious of socialist ideas. It was not until the 1960s that mural art was rediscovered in the United States. Chicanos and African Americans especially found the work of *Los Tres Grandes* to be relevant to many of their own struggles. In Mexico, *muralismo* also enjoyed renewed interest and by 1969 there were almost thirteen hundred murals in the country.

Today, Orozco is considered national patrimony by the Mexican government, and his work is a favorite focus for many exhibitions there. National patrimony means that Orozco's art can only be loaned for exhibition abroad—it cannot leave Mexico permanently. In the United States, his art has been featured at the Museum of Modern Art in New York, at various sites in California, at Dartmouth College in New Hampshire, and many other museums as well. In Europe, Orozco's work has been featured in cities such as Paris, Vienna, Oxford, and Budapest.

It is clear that Orozco made a major impact in the world of art. Even though many of his compositions were inspired directly from Mexican life, the character of Orozco's art was more universal than local in both scope and theme. Mexican writer Teresa Del Conde takes heart when she says that as long as we continue to analyze Orozco's murals, they will tell us something new.[16] Thanks to the enduring quality of fresco painting, we will continue to learn from Orozco's art for many generations to come.

CHRONOLOGY

1883—José Clemente Orozco is born on November 23 in Jalisco, Mexico.

1890—Moves to Mexico City; later, while attending primary school, discovers the printmaking of José Guadalupe Posada and goes to night classes at the San Carlos Academy of Art.

1896—Enrolls in the National School of Agriculture in San Jacinto; graduates three years later with a degree in agricultural engineering.

1897—Suffers an accident that leads to the amputation of his left hand.

1900—Enters the National Preparatory School and specializes in mathematics and architectural drawing.

1911—Works as a political cartoonist for *El Hijo del Ahuizote* and *El Imparcial* in Mexico City.

1913—Completes the *House of Tears Collection*; receives his first government commission.

1915—Travels with the "Red Battalions"; works as a political cartoonist for *La Vanguardia* in Orizaba; meets Margarita Valladares.

1916—Has his first public, one-man exhibition in the Librería Biblos.

1917—Travels to the United States; has much of his art confiscated and destroyed by United States Customs.

1920—Returns to Mexico.

1922— Joins the Syndicate of Revolutionary Technical Workers, Painters, and Sculptors and works as a cartoonist for *El Machete*.

1923— Receives commission to decorate the National Preparatory School. Marries Margarita Valladares.

1924— Is ordered to stop his work at La Prepa after students deface his mural.

1925— Creates mural for The House of Tiles; receives commission to create a fresco at the Industrial School at Orizaba.

1926— Completes fresco at Orizaba and resumes work at La Prepa.

1927— Goes to the United States.

1929— Publishes his first article in English.

1930—Travels to Pomona College in Claremont, California, to create a mural; paints a series of murals at the New School for Social Research in New York City.

1931— Orozco's family joins him in New York.

1932— Arrives in May at Dartmouth College in Hanover, New Hampshire; makes his trip to Europe; in the fall begins an epic work telling the story of the rise of American civilization.

1934— Completes the Dartmouth frescoes and has exhibitions of his work in La Porte, Indiana, and Chicago; returns home to Mexico City where he is commissioned to create a mural in the Palace of Fine Arts.

1936— Decorates the State University of Jalisco in Guadalajara.

1937— Creates the fresco, *Hidalgo and National Independence*, in the Government Palace in Guadalajara, Mexico.

1938— Begins work on the Chapel of the Hospicio Cabañas orphanage.

1939— Finishes murals at the Hospicio Cabañas.

1940—Commissioned by President Cárdenas to take charge of the decoration of the new Mexican Supreme Court; finishes detachable mural, *A Dive Bomber and Tank*, for the Museum of Modern Art in New York; creates murals for the Gabino Ortiz Library in Jiquilpán, Mexico.

1941— Finishes frescoes in Supreme Court Building, Mexico City.

1942— Has autobiography published in *Excelsior* in fifteen installments; begins murals at the Jesús Hospital.

1947— Orozco wins the National Prize in the Arts and Sciences and his work is featured in a one-man show held in the Palace of Fine Arts in Mexico City; illustrates John Steinbeck's *The Pearl*.

1948—Completes outdoor mural at the Teachers College in Mexico City.

1949— Creates *Hidalgo* fresco in the Government Palace in Guadalajara; begins work on a garden mural in a housing project; dies of a heart attack on September 7.

CHAPTER NOTES

CHAPTER 1. TRAGEDY AT A YOUNG AGE

1. José Clemente Orozco, *José Clemente Orozco: An Autobiography* (Austin: University of Texas Press, 1962), p. 9.

2. "Interchangeable Dive Bomber," *The New Yorker*, July 6, 1940, p. 14.

CHAPTER 2. THE BLOSSOMING ARTIST

1. Alma M. Reed, *The Mexican Muralists* (New York: Crown Publishers, Inc., 1960), pp. 42–43.

2. Mexican Artists: *Works by Posada, Orozco, Rivera, and Siqueiros* (Chicago: Allan Frumkin Gallery, 1976), p. 1.

3. MacKinley Helm, *Man of Fire: J. C. Orozco* (Westport, Conn.: Greenwood Press, 1953), p. 8.

4. José Clemente Orozco, *José Clemente Orozco: An Autobiography* (Austin: University of Texas Press, 1962), p. 8.

5. Alma Reed, *Orozco* (New York: Oxford University Press, 1956), p. 21.

6. Ibid.

7. Orozco, p. 9.

8. Jean Charlot, *An Artist on Art* (Honolulu: University of Hawaii Press, 1972), p. 245.

9. Orozco, p. 19.

10. Jean Charlot, *The Mexican Mural Renaissance: 1920–1925* (New Haven: Yale University Press, 1963), p. 35.

11. Orozco, p. 29.

12. Genaro García, *Crónica Oficial de las Fiestas del Primer Centenario*, Mexico, 1911, as quoted in Jean Charlot, "Orozco's Stylistic Evolution," *College Art Journal*, 1949–1950, p. 148.

CHAPTER 3. ¡REVOLUCIÓN!

1. "José Clemente Orozco," *Current Biography* (New York: H. W. Wilson Co., 1940), p. 625.

2. José Clemente Orozco, *José Clemente Orozco: An Autobiography* (Austin: University of Texas Press, 1962), p. 40.

3. Jean Charlot, *Mexican Art and the Academy of San Carlos, 1785–1915* (Austin: University of Texas Press, 1962), p. 160.

4. Alma Reed, *Orozco* (New York: Oxford University Press, 1956), p. 69.

5. José Juan Tablada in *El Mundo Ilustrado*, November 9, 1913, as quoted in Laurance P. Hurlburt, *The Mexican Muralists in the United States* (Albuquerque: University of New Mexico Press, 1989), p. 21.

6. Orozco, p. 54.

7. Bernard S. Myers, *Mexican Painting in Our Time* (New York: Oxford University Press, 1956), p. 45.

8. *Current Biography*, p. 625.

9. Davies, Ivor, "Diego Rivera and Mexican Art," *Studio International*, vol. 200, November 1987, p. 35.

10. Tatiana Herrero Orozco, ed., *Cartas a Margarita* (Mexico: Ediciones Era, 1987), p. 73.

11. Alfred Neumeyer, "Orozco's Mission," *College Art Journal*, Winter 1950–1951, p. 122.

12. José Juan Tablada, "Orozco, the Mexican Goya," *International Studio*, March 1924, p. 500.

13. Thomas Craven, *Modern Art: The Men, the Movements, the Meaning* (New York: Simon & Schuster, 1934), p. 360.

14. Jean Charlot, "Orozco's Stylistic Evolution," *College Art Journal* (1949–1950), p. 151.

15. Jean Charlot, *An Artist on Art* (Honolulu: University of Hawaii Press, 1972), p. 247.

16. José Juan Tablada, "Mexican Painting Today," *International Studio*, January 1923, p. 273–274.

17. Orozco, p. 60.

18. Ibid., p. 61.

19. Ibid., p. 62.

20. Jean Charlot, *The Mexican Mural Renaissance: 1920–1925* (New Haven: Yale University Press, 1963), p. 221.

CHAPTER 4. MEXICO'S GOLDEN AGE

1. Walter Pach, *Queer Thing, Painting* (Freeport, New York: Books for Libraries Press, 1971), p. 285.

2. Margarita Valladares de Orozco, ed., *Cartas a Margarita* (México: Ediciones Era, 1987), p. 20.

3. Ibid., p. 19.

4. Teresa Del Conde, "José Clemente Orozco: En Torno a las 'Cartas a Margarita'," *Anales del Instituto de Investigaciones Estéticas*, vol. 15, no. 58, 1987, p. 119.

5. John Hutton, "'If I am to die tomorrow'—Roots and Meanings of Orozco's *Zapata Entering a Peasants' Hut*," *Museum Studies*, Fall 1984, p. 43.

6. "José Orozco, 65, Mexican Painter," *The New York Times*, September 8, 1949, p. 29.

7. José Clemente Orozco, "Notas Acerca de la Técnica de la Pintura Mural en México en los Ultimos 25 Años," *Exposición Nacional José Clemente Orozco* (Mexico: Secretaria de Educación Pública, 1947), p. 4.

8. E. M. Benson, "Orozco in New England," *American Magazine of Art*, October 1933, p. 449.

9. Alma Reed, *Orozco* (New York: Oxford University Press, 1956), p. 9.

10. Ibid., p. 10.

11. Bernard S. Myers, *Mexican Painting in Our Time* (New York: Oxford University Press, 1956), p. 89.

12. José Clemente Orozco, *José Clemente Orozco: An Autobiography* (Austin: University of Texas Press, 1962), p.8.

13. Laurence E. Schmeckebier, *Modern Mexican Art* (Westport, Conn.: Greenwood Press, 1939), p. 59.

14. Carlos Mérida, *Frescoes in Preparatory School by Orozco, Rivera, and Others* (Mexico City: Frances Toor Studios, 1937), p. 2.

15. Del Conde, p. 120.

16. Tablada, 1924, p. 492.

17. Reed, p. 8.

18. Anita Brenner, *Idols Behind Altars: The Story of the Mexican Spirit* (Boston: Beacon Press, 1929), p. 275.

19. Jean Charlot, "Orozco's Stylistic Evolution," *College Art Journal*, 1949–1950, p. 154.

20. Reed, p. 13.
21. Charlot, "Orozco's Stylistic Evolution," p. 153.
22. Jean Charlot, *The Artist in New York* (Austin: University of Texas Press, 1974), p. 10.
23. Ibid., p. 9.

CHAPTER 5. EL NORTE

1. Jean Charlot, *An Artist on Art* (Honolulu: University of Hawaii Press, 1972), p. 297.
2. Alma Reed, *Orozco* (New York: Oxford University Press, 1956), pp. 49–50.
3. Ibid., pp. 35–36.
4. Ibid., p. 7.
5. Raquel Tibol, "Triste Novela en las Cartas de José Clemente Orozco," *Universidad de Mexico*, April 1987, p. 30.
6. Charlot, *An Artist on Art*, p. 304.
7. José Clemente Orozco, *José Clemente Orozco: An Autobiography* (Austin: University of Texas Press, 1962), pp. 128–129.
8. Orozco's September 25, 1928 letter to Jean Charlot in Charlot, *Artist on Art*, pp. 312–313.
9. Reed, pp. 133–134.
10. Tibol, p. 32.
11. José Clemente Orozco, "New World, New Races, New Art," *Creative Art*, January 29, 1929, p. 135.
12. Reed, p. 178.
13. Teresa Del Conde, "José Clemente Orozco: En Torno a las 'Cartas a Margarita,'" *Anales del Instituto de Investigaciones Estéticas*, vol. 15, no. 58, 1987, p. 115.
14. MacKinley Helm, *Man of Fire: J. C. Orozco* (Westport, Conn.: Greenwood Press, 1953), p. 51.
15. Laurance P. Hurlburt, "Notes on Orozco's North American Murals" in David Elliot, ed., *¡Orozco!* (Oxford: Museum of Modern Art, 1980), p. 43.
16. Alvin Johnson, *Notes on the New School Murals* (New York: New School for Social Research), p. 11.
17. Bernard S. Myers, *Mexican Painting in Our Time* (New York: Oxford University Press, 1956), p. 105.
18. Johnson, p. 11.

19. Hurlburt, p. 268.

20. John Hutton, "'If I am to die tomorrow'—Roots and Meanings of Orozco's *Zapata Entering a Peasant's Hut*," *Museum Studies*, Fall 1984, p. 40.

CHAPTER 6. THE ARTIST IN NEW ENGLAND

1. MacKinley Helm, *Man of Fire: J. C. Orozco* (Westport, Conn.: Greenwood Press, 1953), p. 56.

2. Albert I. Dickerson, *Orozco Frescoes at Dartmouth* (Hanover, N.H.: Dartmouth College, 1962), p. 4.

3. Laurance P. Hurlburt, "Notes on Orozco's North American Murals" as quoted in David Elliot, ed., *¡Orozco!* (Oxford: Museum of Modern Art, 1980), p. 54.

4. Tatiana Herrero Orozco, ed., *Cartas a Margarita* (Mexico: Ediciones Era, 1987), pp. 26–27.

5. Lewis Mumford, "Orozco in New England," *The New Republic*, October 10, 1934, p. 233.

6. Bernard S. Myers, *Mexican Painting in Our Time* (New York: Oxford University Press, 1956), p. 112.

7. Joyce Waddell Bailey, "José Clemente Orozco (1883–1949): Formative Years in the Narrative Graphic Tradition," *Latin American Research Review*, vol. 15, no. 3, 1980, p. 85.

8. Mumford, p. 232.

9. "José Clemente Orozco," *Current Biography* (New York: H. W. Wilson Co., 1940), p. 625.

10. Mumford, p. 235.

11. Churchill P. Lathrop as quoted in Harris and Lyon, p. 60.

12. Laurance P. Hurlburt, *The Mexican Muralists in the United States* (Albuquerque: University of New Mexico Press, 1989), p. 87.

CHAPTER 7. BACK HOME

1. James D. Egleson, "José Clemente Orozco," *Parnassus*, November 1940, p. 9.

2. David Elliot, ed., *¡Orozco!* (Oxford: Museum of Modern Art, 1980), p. 87.

3. Alma Reed, *Orozco* (New York: Oxford University Press, 1956), p. 59.

4. Alfred Neumeyer, "Orozco's Mission," *College Art Journal*, Winter 1950–1951, p. 127.

5. Desmond Rochfort, *The Mexican Muralists* (New York: Universe Publishing, 1993), p. 111.

6. Egleson, p. 9.

7. Neumeyer, p. 125.

8. MacKinley Helm, *Man of Fire: J. C. Orozco* (Westport, Conn.: Greenwood Press, 1953), p. 87.

9. "Orozco's New Job," *Arts Digest*, July 1940, p. 26.

10. Helm, p. 84.

11. "Orozco Completes Fresco at Museum," *The New York Times*, July 4, 1940, p. 13.

12. *Bulletin of the Museum of Modern Art*, August 1940, as quoted in Bernard S. Myers, *Mexican Painting in Our Time* (New York: Oxford University Press, 1956), p. 166.

CHAPTER 8. A PRODUCTIVE LIFE

1. Alvin Johnson, *Notes on the New School Murals* (New York: The International Press), p. 9.

2. MacKinley Helm, *Man of Fire: J. C. Orozco* (Westport, Conn.: Greenwood Press, 1953), p. 90.

3. José Clemente Orozco, *José Clemente Orozco: An Autobiography* (Austin: University of Texas Press, 1962), p. 3.

4. Helm, p. 92.

5. Tatiana Herrera Orozco, ed., *Cartas a Margarita* (Mexico: Ediciones Era, 1987), p. 40.

6. Wallace S. Baldinger, "Orozco's Last Murals," *Magazine of Art*, February 1950, p. 44.

7. Baldinger, p. 43.

8. Helm, p. 105.

9. Herrera Orozco, p. 47.

10. Ibid., p. 106.

11. Helm, p. 106.

12. Justino Fernández, "Orozco, Genius of America," *College Art Journal*, Winter 1949–1950, p. 142.

13. "Dos Días de Duelo Nacional Decretó Ayer la Cámara," *Excelsior*, September 9, 1949, p. 1.

CHAPTER 9. HIS LEGACY, HIS ART

1. "José Clemente Orozco," *Current Biography* (New York: H. W. Wilson Co., 1940), p. 626.
2. Alfred Neumeyer, "Orozco's Mission," *College Art Journal*, Winter 1950–1951, p. 121.
3. Justino Fernández, "Orozco, Genius of America," *College Art Journal*, Winter 1949–1950, p. 142.
4. Octavio Paz, "Social Realism: The Murals of Rivera, Orozco, and Siqueiros," *Arts Canada*, December–January 1979–1980, p. 64.
5. Jean Charlot, *An Artist on Art* (Honolulu: University of Hawaii Press, 1972), p. 239.
6. Charles Giuliano, "Orozco's American Epic," *Art News*, November 1989, p. 55.
7. "Orozco Completes New York Frescoes and the Critics Criticize," *The Art Digest*, February 15, 1931, p. 9.
8. Lloyd Goodrich, "The Murals of the New School," *The Arts*, March 1931, p. 444.
9. Alma Reed, *Orozco* (New York: Oxford University Press, 1956), p. 302.
10. Kimball Flaccus, *Orozco at Dartmouth* (Hanover, N.H.: The Arts Press, 1933), p. viii.
11. Laurence E. Schmeckebier, *Modern Mexican Art* (Westport, Conn.: Greenwood Press, 1939), p. 106.
12. Albert I. Dickerson, ed., *Orozco Frescoes at Dartmouth* (Hanover, N.H.: Dartmouth College, 1962), p. 1.
13. Augusto Orea Marín, *Orozco: El Mito* (Jalisco, Mexico: Editorial Conexión Gráfica, 1994), p. 21.
14. Reed, p. 196.
15. Peter Yates, "Tribute to a Giant," *California Arts and Architecture*, January 1943, p. 34.
16. Del Conde, p. 111.

FURTHER READING

Charlot, Jean. *The Artist in New York*. Austin: University of Texas Press, 1974.

———. *The Mexican Mural Renaissance: 1920–1925*. New Haven: Yale University Press, 1963.

Gonzales, Doreen. *Diego Rivera: His Art, His Life*. Springfield, N.J.: Enslow Publishers, Inc., 1996.

Helm, MacKinley. *Man of Fire: J. C. Orozco*. Westport, Conn.: Greenwood Press, 1953.

Hurlburt, Laurance P. *The Mexican Muralists in the United States*. Albuquerque: University of New Mexico Press, 1991.

Janson, Dora J. *Story of Painting*. New York: Harry N. Abrams, Inc., 1976.

Myers, Bernard S. *Mexican Painting in Our Time*. New York: Oxford University Press, 1956.

Orozco, José Clemente. *José Clemente Orozco: An Autobiography*. Austin: University of Texas Press, 1962.

Reed, Alma M. *The Mexican Muralists*. New York: Crown Publishers, Inc., 1960.

———. *Orozco*. New York: Oxford University Press, 1956.

Rochfort, Desmond. *Mexican Muralists: Orozco, Rivera, Siqueiros*. San Francisco: Chronicle Books, 1998.

Stein, R. Conrad. *The Mexican Revolution, 1910–1920*. Parsippany, N.J.: Silver Burdett Press, 1994.

INDEX

A

Academy of Fine Arts of San Carlos, 15, 17, 18, 20, 25, 27, 35
Anglo-America, 78–79
Ashram, 58–59, 62
Atl, Dr. *See* Murillo, Gerardo.

C

Carranza, Venustiano, 27, 69
Casa de Azulejos (House of Tiles), 47, 49
Catharsis, 84
Charlot, Jean, 49, 53, 54, 55, 60, 107
Christ Burning His Cross, 42
Christ Chopping Down His Own Cross, 43
The Coming of Quetzalcoatl, 77–78
Cortés and Malinche, 52
Creative Man, 85

D

Damas Católicas (Catholic Ladies), 43–44, 62
Dartmouth College, 72, 74, 75, 80, 82, 86, 108
Delphic Studios, 62, 63
Desastres de la Guerra (Disasters of War), 87, 89
The Destruction of the Old Order, 52
A Dive Bomber and Tank, 89–91, 92, 93
drawings, 53, 54, 57, 61, 95, 112

E

El Hijo del Ahuizote (The Son of the Ahuizote), 24
El Machete, 36
Enseñanza (Teaching), 62

F

False Justice, 94
Fernando R. Galván & Company, 32
The Franciscan and the Indian, 42
frescoes. *See* murals.

G

Galván, Fernando R., 32
Gods of the Modern World, 79–80
Government Palace in Guadalajara, 85, 100
Guadalajara, Mexico, 11, 20, 84, 85, 86, 87, 94, 100

H

House of Tears, 26, 29–30, 57

I

Industrial School at Orizba, 49
Iturbe, Don Francisco Sergio, 47, 49

L

La Vanguardia, 27, 28, 53
Los Horrores de la Revolución (The Horrors of the Revolution), 53, 57
Los Tres Grandes (The Big Three), 39, 113

M

Man of Fire, 86

Man Released from the Mechanistic, 74
Maternity, 42, 43, 44
Mexican Mural Renaissance, 38–39
Mexican Revolution, 23–24, 31, 33, 34, 51, 52, 53, 60, 61, 66, 69
Mexico City, Mexico, 7, 8, 13, 25, 29, 30, 34, 35, 47, 58, 69, 92, 93, 95, 96, 98, 101
Mexico in Revolution, 61
Miguel Alemán housing complex, 101
Modern Human Sacrifice, 78
Modern Industrial Man, 80
The Mother's Farewell, 52
murals, 39–44, 45, 46–47, 49, 51–52, 55, 62, 64–65, 66, 74, 75, 77–80, 82, 84–85, 86–87, 89–91, 94, 95–96, 98–99, 100, 101, 108–110, 112, 113–114
Murillo, Gerardo, 20–21, 27, 28

N

National Allegory, 99–100
National Preparatory School (La Prepa), 18, 39, 41, 42, 43, 44, 46, 47, 49, 51, 52, 62
New School for Social Research, 65–66, 68, 69, 94, 108

O

Omnisciencia, 49
Orozco, Ireneo (father), 11, 18
Orozco, José Clemente
   art exhibitions, 29–30, 60, 61, 63, 69, 89, 98
   autobiography, 24–25, 95
   awards, 98
   birth, 11
   childhood, 7–9, 13, 15, 17–18
   children, 45, 62, 103
   death, 103–105
   education, 13, 15, 17, 18, 20
   Europe, trip to, 75
   gunpowder explosion, 8–9, 17, 18, 112
   marriage, 44
   newspaper cartoonist, 24, 27–28, 29, 34, 38, 47, 53
   teaching at Dartmouth, 72–75
   United States, 31–33, 55, 56–62, 63–66, 68–69, 71, 72–75, 77–80, 82, 89–92
Orozco, Luis (brother), 13
Orozco, Margarita Valladares (wife), 28–29, 35–36, 44–45, 58, 60, 62, 65, 71, 75, 84, 93, 96, 98, 103, 108, 112
Orozco, Rosa (sister), 13
Orozco, Rosa Flores (mother), 11, 13, 15, 17, 44, 60, 84
Orozco y Valladares, Alfredo Leonardo (son), 45, 62, 103
Orozco y Valladares, Clemente Humberto (son), 45, 62, 103
Orozco y Valladares, Eugenia Lucrecia (daughter), 45, 62, 103

P

paintings, 26, 29–30, 31, 57, 62, 69, 71
Palacio de Bellas Artes (Palace of Fine Arts), 83, 98, 105
Posada, José Guadalupe, 13, 15, 79, 89, 112
Primavera (Spring), 101
Prometheus, 65
Pruneda, Dr. Alfonso, 51, 52

R

Reed, Alma, 42, 58, 59, 62, 110
The Return of Quetzalcoatl, 77, 78
Rivera, Diego, 36, 39, 83, 105, 112

S

Siqueiros, David Alfaro, 32–33,
    36, 39, 46, 47, 105, 112
*Social, Political, and Aesthetic
    Declaration*, 36
Social Revolution, 49, 51
The Strike, 66
Struggle in the Occident, 66, 68
*Surrender by the Spaniards at
    San Juan de Ulúa in 1822*,
    26
Syndicate of Revolutionary
    Technical Workers, Painters,
    and Sculptors, 36, 47

T

Table of Brotherhood, 66, 68
Tzontemoc, 42

U

The Universal Family, 66

V

Vasconcelos, José, 38, 39, 42, 46

Z

Zapata Entering a Peasant's Hut,
    69, 71